An Incomplete Guide to Using Counselling Skills on the Telephone

2nd Edition

Pete Sanders

PCCS BOOKS
Manchester

First Edition Published in 1993
Second Edition Published 1996
PCCS BOOKS
Paragon House
Manchester
M16 0LN

An Incomplete Guide to Using Counselling Skills on the Telephone

ISBN   1 898059 12 8 (paperback)
          1 898059 13 6 (hardback)

Cover design by PCCS Books and Create Publications, Bath.
Printed by Redwood Books, Trowbridge, Wilts.

Contents

Contents

Contents

Introduction to the Second Edition

The second edition of this book was 'forced' upon me for a few reasons. Communications technology has moved quickly in four years, telephone helping has developed into a sophisticated branch of counselling and counselling skills, and not least, the first edition was so popular.

It now seems a long time since I started to write the first edition and since it was the first book I had written, I could find twenty ways of improving it as soon as the manuscript left my hands. I hope that my increased confidence shows in this second edition. There are new chapters and much of the old material has been re-worked and added to - it is very much a 'revised' edition.

Those readers familiar with the first edition will notice changes to the *In Training* panels. Not all panels have a *Method* and *Learning points* section, since the learning points for some activities were, I felt, obvious. The chapter on research is there more to encourage agencies to conduct or commission evaluations and research than it is to give examples of good work. This is explained in the chapter.

This book contains contributions from Frances McDonnell and Anna Karczewska, for which I am grateful. I hope that the contemporary experiences of helpline workers will give some added depth to the reader's experience.

Finally, I don't feel uncomfortable about thanking the most important people in my life, namely my immediate family; Maggie, Jake, Rosie, Hannah and Sam. They had to do without me whilst I was working and I would not have been able to get this work done without their support. Also, I had invaluable help with proof-reading from Stella Lancaster.

Pete Sanders
Manchester
January 1996

1   Useful Questions

The Most Useful Question

As counsellors and helpers we are used to doing our business face-to-face. Unless we are born without sight we learn nearly all of our relationship skills through our primary sense of vision and many counselling texts refer to the special role of sight in 'active listening'. In fact counsellors pride themselves on the quality of this person-to-person contact.

When thinking about counselling on the telephone most people, including many experienced counsellors, go glassy eyed and muse about differences, difficulties and complications. We get distracted when the familiar ingredients in our tried and trusted counselling recipes are taken away. It reminds me of asking for a vegetarian meal in a restaurant 15 years ago and getting meat and two veg without the meat. Do we offer the same to our telephone clients?

During a workshop on telephone skills I wondered why our counselling marbles fly straight out of the window when we lose visual contact with our clients, that is, every time we pick up the phone. So we brainstormed the most common issues that arise around telephone work. As we 'stormed' and scribbled on our flipchart one question kept cropping up again and again. As each pitfall and issue concerning telephone work was highlighted, the same question returned in our minds and on our flipcharts. We soon realised that this was The Most Useful Question we could ask ourselves.

It was so simple and obvious. It led our thinking somewhere positive in every case. It untangled knots all over the place. Whether the problem was what to do with people who wanted us to talk to them while they masturbated; what to do when clients go silent; what to do with 'hoaxers'; third party calls, or what the limits of confidentiality are in the 'real world', the same question helped us get our counselling marbles back in place, and our thinking back on track.

The Most Useful Question is:

What would I do in this situation if it were face-to-face?

We played for ages with this question. It helped us look at issues from a perspective which wasn't clouded by telephone terror, it gave an extra dimension to our discussion and it had its funny side when applied to popular 'telephone teasers'. Try it yourself for a bit before moving on to some more useful questions. Try it in training sessions, when discussing professional or ethical issues in telephone work and try asking yourself this question when you get in a tight spot on the phone with a client.

More Useful Questions (but not quite as useful as The Most Useful Question)

What are the advantages of telephone counselling?

Perhaps you haven't thought about the advantages of telephone counselling before. Take a moment to think about the question.

In Training: Most of us think that telephone work is 'second best' so it is a good idea to explore the possibility that it might have positive benefits.

Method:

• Split the group into threes or fours and ask them to brainstorm answers to the above question.

• Feedback and collate answers, then discuss.

Learning points: The ideas on the following page or two can be used to stimulate or focus discussion on the advantages of telephone helping over face-to-face work.

As I suggested in the training panel above, most people immediately make the assumption that the telephone is somehow second best or that real counselling can only be done face-to-face. Indeed, many agencies have specific policies which implicitly accept, support and promote this assumption. They instruct volunteers to talk to callers only as long as it takes to persuade (in a non-directive way of course!) the caller to visit the agency's premises for face-to-face counselling. Many volunteers (and callers) soon pick up the message that the phone is somehow not good enough for this kind of helping. This kind of attitude then limits the degree to which we explore the skills of telephone helping properly and take them seriously. Telephone skills and telephone helping is not an aperitif before the main course; it is increasingly becoming the only meal we offer clients, so we will look at the benefits to both us and them.

What *are* the advantages? They very much depend upon your personal circumstances, the type of service that the agency is offering and the financial constraints of the service. Some advantages benefit clients, whilst others benefit counsellors or agencies. If you haven't already tried the training activity on the facing page, here are a few advantages to doing helping on the phone. It's not supposed to be a complete list, just a few ideas to get you thinking, though there may well be further advantages relating to your particular agency and its circumstances.

Benefits to the client
• Convenient for client.
• Better access for some disadvantaged groups.
• Cheaper than face-to-face for client.
• Client is not seen, and is therefore anonymous.

Benefits to the agency
• Needs less accommodation.
• Doesn't necessarily need an appointments system.
• Location and environment of premises are seen as less important.
• Better personal safety for counsellors.
• Counsellor anonymity, if required.
• Counsellor can make notes as a memory aid.

Why do people choose to use telephone counselling services rather than see a counsellor face-to-face?

In Training:
Method:
• Split the group into threes and fours then ask them to brainstorm answers to the question above.
• Feedback and collate answers then discuss.
Learning Points:
• This can be a good exercise to increase awareness of clients' experiences and their lives in general. In other words it will help improve our capacity to offer empathy (see Chapter 6, page 81).

There are several *external* reasons why people may choose the telephone. By 'external' I mean some obstacle which lies outside the control of the individual. Some people do not have the flexibility and freedom in their lives to visit a counsellor. Such individuals and groups may include:
• Single parents and those with young children and no childcare.
• People with a disability.
• Older people who may be afraid of going into busy town centres.
• People living in remote areas.
• People caring for disabled or infirm relatives.
• Those who find transport difficult.
• Those whose personal freedom is restricted by another person such as abused women or children.
• People on a low income or in receipt of state support may find that transport costs are higher than the price of a 30 minute phone call.

There are also some *internal* or psychological reasons why people may choose the telephone. For various reasons these people feel unable to visit a face-to-face agency or specialist individual:
• Counsellors are very concerned to offer a relationship that is as near to a partnership of equals as can be achieved. Most agencies

offering counselling services, telephone or otherwise, try to make this very clear in their publicity. Yet we all know that out there in the 'real world' many people just do not know what we are offering. For such people, using the telephone is a low-risk way of testing the counsellor (and counselling) out.

• For some people, going to a counsellor would carry too much social stigma for them to bear or they might feel that it would be too great a sign of weakness. The telephone gives some power back to such people. They may feel more in control if they can remain anonymous or put the receiver down and withdraw from the session without embarrassment or explanation.

• Others may not want to be 'seen'. Perhaps they suffer from acute social embarrassment or they cannot face the thought of their 'problem' being made visible (even to themselves) by declaring it in the presence of another person. The telephone affords a more comfortable halfway house for these people.

• Some people are just too frightened to *go* to a doctor, counsellor or agency for help. They need the security that being able to use the telephone (possibly in the safety of their own home) gives them. The telephone is a safe way of making contact with strangers or specialist helpers without actually having to *meet* them.

Are there any disadvantages to telephone counselling?
If you are still of the opinion that it's vital to be in the same room as the person you're trying to help, then here is your chance, and it's an opportunity to say how important all of those visual cues are.

In Training: It is important to get all angles on telephone work so that advantages can be exploited and weaknesses allowed for.
Method:
• Again, split the group into threes and fours then brainstorm answers to the question above.
• Feedback and collate answers then discuss.

Face-to-face, sighted counselling *is different* from telephone counselling, and telephone work does have its disadvantages. I'll leave you to fill in the details on the obvious first disadvantage:
- The counsellor and client cannot make visual contact.
- The caller can terminate the session at any time and may do this impulsively to avoid tackling important issues.
- There are potentially more distractions and interruptions when working on the phone, for both the client and the counsellor.
- It's not possible to ensure the client's privacy on the phone.

How does telephone counselling differ from face-to-face counselling ?

Again, it's a rather obvious point to make, but you can't see who you're talking to on the phone. This gives rise to a number of special considerations regarding telephone work. Also, the telephone gives a different set of 'relationship tools' to those making the call than we are accustomed to in face-to-face interactions. This creates another set of special considerations. These can be looked at in two sets:

1. Differences due to the fact that you can't see who you're talking to:
- *Client anonymity*

Every time the phone rings, the counsellor never knows whether they have spoken to the caller before or not. It might be a regular client or a first interview. This is in contrast to all but the most drop-in of face-to-face services.

- *Confidentiality*

Confidentiality is an issue in all counselling settings, and in telephone counselling at the moment (technological advances may soon change this) both the client and counsellor can have complete control over their identities and their location. The caller can remain anonymous throughout the relationship if they so choose.

- *Helper anonymity*

Counsellors and helpers can also remain anonymous. Indeed this is often a requirement in many agencies. A counsellor may find this an awkward boundary which may get in the way of them forming a good relationship with their client. Other counsellors may feel more secure and relaxed in this anonymity.

• *First impressions*
The two points above have an effect on both client and counsellor judgements, since we form some very durable impressions on first *sight*. Economic status, social class, gender, racial origin etc. are all things we are likely to make guesses (sometimes very bad guesses) about as a result of how people look.

• *Auditory cues*
When we can't see the person we are talking to we use a different set of cues, those that we can hear (auditory cues). Such things as accent, dialect, tone of voice, pitch of voice etc. come to the fore in helping us make judgements about the person we are trying to help. Some of these judgements we make on first *hearing* may be completely different from those we make at first *sight*.

In Training: It can be useful to look at the effects of auditory cues in order to demonstrate how powerful they are.
Method:
• Play a tape of different people saying a fixed sentence then getting small groups of trainees to give each voice a 'life story' with lots of demographic detail - name, age, gender, job (or not), hobbies, ethnic origin, sexual orientation, etc.
• Vary the exercise by using voices with very different qualities, accents, etc.
• Share the 'life stories' of each of the small groups in the large group and then discuss.
Learning Points:
• Our prejudices regarding social class, ethnicity and sexuality may well come out in this exercise. Be prepared for a vigorous discussion and be prepared to challenge sexist, racist and homophobic views.

• *Expectations*

Probably the greatest influence on our behaviour is the set of expectations we bring to each situation. If we expect working on the telephone to be harder or more problematic than face-to-face helping, then it probably will be. The same goes for the person we are trying to help.

• *Effort*

Telephone counselling can require more concentration than face-to-face counselling because the counsellor is working 'blind' and has to work with a more limited range of cues. This extra effort can make the whole business much more exhausting than face-to-face work. (See Chapters 3, 7 & 9)

Differences due to a new set of 'relationship tools':

When I talk about 'relationship tools', I mean those factors that we use in the management of relationships which rely on us being, for example, in the same room as the other person, or the rules of politeness or courtesy which have grown up with telephone use. Also we have a history in our culture of using the phone as a 'quick-fix' solution, or message channel when face-to-face contact can't be achieved. Sometimes it is seen, as I have already mentioned, as a second best option. This affects some of the ways we use counselling skills on the phone and some of the ways clients behave:

• *Control*

In telephone counselling the counsellor has less control over some aspects of the relationship than in face-to-face counselling. On the phone, clients can virtually start and stop the session when they please.

• *Length of 'session'*

In most face-to-face counselling settings, the sessions are of a roughly predetermined length, whereas in most telephone counselling settings the call is of variable length and may in some agencies be unlimited. (Some agencies have a policy that ensures that only the client can terminate contact. This can lead to some very long calls. See Chapter 7)

• *Number of sessions*
Many telephone counselling relationships can be one call only.
The caller is likely to call once and never again. Face-to-face
relationships more often last for a few sessions spread over some
weeks, and occasionally many sessions over a period of months.
Telephone work is much shorter term, with a relationship lasting
weeks or months being the exception rather than the rule.

• *Caller expectations*
The client may expect the telephone service offered by an agency
or individual as a preliminary to the 'real' face-to-face counselling.
This means that they may never really get started, preferring to
leave the 'real stuff' for the face-to-face session.

Possibly the Most Important Question:
Is it <u>possible</u> to do counselling on the telephone?
You will of course realise that the title of this book is *'An Incomplete
Guide to Using Counselling **Skills** on the Telephone'*, not
*'...**Counselling** on the Telephone'*. There is, however, a body of
opinion which never seems to consider the possibility that *counselling*
can take place in anything other than face-to-face contexts and
others which actually build in face-to-face contact as a requirement
in their definition of counselling. This question is so important that
I have devoted a whole chapter to it, Chapter 3, but for the moment
we will review the issues briefly.

One reason why I have left this question until last is because the
answer is, to some extent, tied up with the next chapter in which I
look at some definitions of ways of helping, including using
counselling skills and counselling. I am tempted to say that if we
can define counselling and identify its key ingredients, then as long
as being face-to-face with the client isn't one of them, we simply
must be able to do it on the phone.

I sometimes have to remind myself that a couple of the best
counsellors I know are blind or visually challenged. How do *they* do
it if sighted, face-to-face contact is a requirement? I have spent the
current chapter asserting that being unsighted is not the only difference

between telephone and face-to-face counselling, so perhaps some definitions of counselling would have other objections to the telephone. If they do, then I haven't come across them yet. It could be that some of the disadvantages to telephone work listed in this chapter have convinced you that bona fide counselling cannot be achieved on the telephone.

I have found Stephen Murgatroyd's book *'Counselling and Helping'* very good for clarifying some issues. He says that it's the idea of what the *nature of the helping is* that should guide our thinking on definitions. He points out that we should not think that 'counselling is what counsellors do', rather that counselling is a certain form of helping with certain aims and possible outcomes. These aims can be held, and these outcomes achieved, by a wide range of people. I would add to that 'in a wide range of situations, *including over the telephone'*.

One set of elements which do separate counselling from most other types of helping is the ethical positions and professional standards within, and towards, which counsellors choose to work. Again, I have neither read nor experienced anything yet which leads me to believe that the telephone might compromise my work ethically or professionally. That doesn't mean to say that the telephone hasn't provided me with many ethical challenges, but none that supervision has failed to cope with to date. This aspect is also given fuller coverage in Chapter 9.

In Training : It is essential that agencies know whether they are attempting to train helpers to do counselling or use counselling skills and the issues surrounding this work. This may help open discussion.
Method:
• Split group into threes and fours and ask the question: 'Is it an essential condition of *counselling* that the counsellor and client have to, a) be able to see the client or, b) be in the same room as the client?'
• Feed back, collate answers and discuss.

2 Necessary Definitions

Why the need to look at definitions?
At some point it's always useful to define the terms we're using and it has become increasingly important over recent years to define all manner of helping activities. Increasing awareness about standards of help, better training and qualifications and an impetus to make counselling into a profession have been relentlessly driving us all to think more about what we actually do when we try to help someone. Definitions of helping should be of concern to everyone from a volunteer in a telephone agency, through helpline workers, to fully fledged telephone counsellors. I do believe it is possible to do telephone counselling rather than use counselling skills on the phone to support some other kind of helping activity, but more of this later in this chapter.

If you thought you could keep your head down and ignore all of this frantic defining that's going on, National Vocational Qualifications (NVQs) will be along soon in a helping relationship near you to bring you back to the 'real' world. Everyone involved in helping, whether telephone based or face-to-face will have to consider carefully the skills that they use and how they use them. Before NVQs made an appearance in the world of catering and food preparation, hygiene standards in sandwich shops and corner cafes were largely a matter of chance. Now everyone handling food has to have a Basic Food Hygiene Certificate as evidence that they are competent to store, prepare and sell food safely. We may be heading the same way in the helping professions with a move in the voluntary sector towards competent practitioner-volunteers rather than kind-hearted but ineffective do-gooders.

Counselling and other forms of helping
Counselling has become one of the most over-used, variously (and

often poorly) defined and misunderstood terms in the past 20 years. It has been used to describe any kind of tutorial or advice situation in education, through various psychotherapies and helping relationships to disciplinary hearings. In the forces and in some medical settings you are said to have been 'counselled' when you have been cautioned or ticked off!

In Training: A popular way to start a counselling skills training programme is to ask trainees to define counselling. *Method:*
• If the group is large, split up into smaller groups of around three or four.
• Ask the groups to brainstorm the meaning of the word 'counselling' for them.
• Collate the definitions or key words/concepts on a flip chart. Then discuss.
• Repeat the exercise using information giving, advice, guidance or befriending, etc. (See below.)
Learning Points:
• Defining the activity is important because we need to put boundaries around activities sometimes and counselling is one of those activities. We need to know its rough position in the 'helping world' before we can put those boundaries in place. We need to know whether we are giving information, counselling, using counselling skills, advising, or befriending at any given time.
• You could also look at other helping roles in everyday life such as friend, parent, nurse, youth worker taken from the experience of the group and compare these with the service you are offering.

So how can we distinguish and separate counselling from other forms of helping relationships?   What are the particular features of counselling?   What are the differences between counselling and counselling skills? Is there only one type of counselling?

There are several sources we can turn to for help with these questions, but there should be a government health warning for all those trying to sort out the tangle of statements released by various bodies and groups. I will try to offer some short cuts, but I do recommend that individuals and groups do the exercise themselves if they are committed to offering helping relationships over a long period of time. As each year goes by, the 'helping professions' (and I would include all manner of voluntary helping within this term) are being forced to become more specific about the helping they are offering, more ethical and proper in their behaviour, more highly trained and better supported in terms of personal and professional backup. Do not get left behind by failing to set high enough standards at the outset. You should try to work out just what sort of helping relationship you are offering. When you are clear about this, the people you are trying to help will be able to use your services to much better effect.

In 1992 the then Advice, Guidance and Counselling Lead Body (now called the Advice, Guidance, Counselling and Psychotherapy Lead Body, or AGC&PLB) published their Differentiation Project Report and Summary Report. The purpose of the project was to map out and explain the differences between various forms of helping activity such as Information Giving, Advice, Guidance, Use of Counselling Skills and Counselling.

The summary report concluded that there were identifiable differences between certain helping activities, such as:

Advising helps the client develop problem solving, increase choices, options and possible actions by providing information appropriate to the client's needs.
Guiding gives the client access to the increased options and information (above in advising) and enables the client to make informed choices by exploring their concerns and developing decision making skills.
In **Befriending** we provide support to distressed people for as long as it may be required. A befriending relationship has an 'everyday' quality to it and will help the person feel more supported and less isolated.

The terms **Mentoring and Tutoring** refer to activities within an educational setting which are concerned with:

i) providing a safe and supportive learning environment,

ii) enabling a learner, student or trainee to construct and manage their own learning environment to meet their own individual learning needs, or

iii) advising or guiding the student within that student-managed learning environment.

There are two important things for us to remember, firstly that our current interest is in how a range of helping activities (including some or all of the above) may be best delivered over the telephone, and secondly that *none of the above is counselling*. At best we may conclude that they would all be enhanced by the application of counselling skills. So what is the difference between counselling and the use of counselling skills?

Counselling and counselling skills

It is clear that the skills involved in counselling can be used by many people who are not counsellors in many situations which are not counselling. Some counselling skills are looked at in much greater detail in Chapter 6 and if you want more help with counselling skills I have suggested some further reading on page 194.

The problem of differentiating between counselling and the use of counselling skills has plagued the counselling profession for years. It seems it is much easier to define counselling (and heaven knows we can agonise over that if given half a chance) rather than identifying the limits of the use of counselling skills, so that is where I will start.

First of all a couple of quotes to get us going. The British Association for Counselling say in their Code of Ethics and Practice for Counsellors (September 1993):

> *"The term 'counselling' includes work with individuals, pairs or groups of people, often, but not always, referred to as 'clients'.*
>
> *Counselling may be concerned with developmental issues, addressing and resolving specific problems, making decisions,*

coping with crisis, developing personal insight and knowledge, working through feelings of inner conflict or improving relationships with others. The counsellor's role is to facilitate the client's work in ways which respect the client's values, personal resources and capacity for self-determination.

Only when both the user and recipient explicitly agree to enter into a counselling relationship does it become 'counselling' rather than the use of 'counselling skills'."

Francesca Inskipp, in her 'Counselling: The Trainer's Handbook', defines counselling as:

"a) providing help and support and an understanding listener for someone who is concerned or perplexed;
b) creating a climate so that the 'client' feels accepted, non-defensive and able to talk freely about himself and his feelings (begins to build a trusting relationship);
c) helping the client to gain clearer insight into himself and his situation so that he is better able to help himself and draw on his resources."
(p 21)

I suggest that there are three elements needed in any definition of counselling:
    i) the *process* of the helping, i.e. what is actually happening,
    ii) the *context* in which the process takes place, and
    iii) the *people* engaged in the helping process.
All three components are required before the activity can be properly named.

I have mentioned in Chapter 1 that Stephen Murgatroyd suggests that it may be important to focus on the nature of the helping process rather than the qualifications or professional standing of the helper. In the same way that healing is the process of being made well and not just the thing that happens to you when you go to a healer, then counselling is the *process* whereby:
    • clients are given an opportunity to explore and discover ways of living more resourcefully,
    • clients are assisted in their own exploration of their world,

• clients are helped to explore their understanding of things that are troubling them,

• clients are enabled to achieve a greater sense of self-determination.
This process could conceivably happen in a number of settings, including over the telephone.

The features which make a counselling *context* particular are:

• The participants must be in psychological contact. (Some helping activities can be done by post for example, but not counselling)

• Both counsellor and client must identify the process as *counselling* rather than some other helping relationship, i.e. befriending, advice or guidance.

• Counselling is freely entered into by the person seeking help, i.e. they are not forced to be there against their will, or held under any threat.

• The counsellor acknowledges the central role of, and actively uses, relationship variables in the counselling process.

• The counsellor will share with the client the common key purpose of the activity, i.e. to help the client by counselling.

The people necessary before we can say that counselling is taking place are, without sounding too silly about it, a counsellor and a client:

• At least two people are required. One must identify themselves as in need of help (the client) the other must identify themselves as the person providing help (the counsellor).

• The counsellor should be competent, i.e. should have appropriate qualifications. For this we can look at the BAC requirements for the recognition of counsellor training courses which recommends amongst other things a minimum of 450 hours training.

• The counsellor should be working within and bound by a professional code of ethics, such as the one governing members of the BAC (Code of Ethics and Practice for Counsellors).

Briefly, to summarise some of the above points, we could say that counselling is practised by a qualified counsellor within a code of ethics, in the service of a client who has freely entered into a relationship that they understand to be counselling, with the aim of helping the client live a more fulfilling life. The use of counselling skills, on the other hand, refers to how we might use some or all of the skills that counsellors use in support of a different set of aims in a different context with different people operating to different codes of ethics.

The BAC publish a Code of Ethics and Practice for Counselling Skills which is prefaced by the following to help practitioners decide for themselves whether they are counselling or using counselling skills:

'B.   The Meaning of Counselling

1.1 The term 'counselling skills' does not have a single definition which is universally accepted. For the purpose of this code, 'counselling skills' are distinguished from 'listening skills' and from 'counselling'. Although the distinction is not always a clear one, because the term 'counselling skills' contains elements of these other two activities, it has its own place in the continuum between them. What distinguishes the use of counselling skills from these other two activities are the intentions of the user, which is to enhance the performance of their functional role, as line manager, nurse, tutor, social worker, personnel officer, voluntary worker, etc., the recipient will, in turn, perceive them in that role.

1.2 Ask yourself the following questions:
a) Are you using counselling skills to enhance your communication with someone but without taking on the role of their counsellor?
b) Does the recipient perceive you as acting within your professional/caring role (which is NOT that of being their counsellor)?
i. If the answer is YES to both these questions, you are using counselling skills in your functional role and should use this document.
ii. If the answer is NO to both, you are counselling and should look to the Code of Ethics & Practice for Counsellors for guidance.
iii. If the answer is YES to one and NO to the other, you have a conflict of expectations and should resolve it.
Only when both the user and the recipient explicitly contract to enter into a counselling relationship does it cease to be 'using

counselling skills and become 'counselling' When this occurs, the
Code of Ethics & Practice for Counsellors should be referred to.'
BAC Code of Ethics and Practice for Counselling Skills (1989)

In Training: It is important that trainees are familiar with the notion of codes of ethics.

Method:

• If the group is large, split up into smaller groups of around three or four.

• Ask the groups to discuss their personal ethics; do they, for example, think that loyalty to friends is important, or that proctecting others is important?

• Collate the definitions or key words/concepts on a flip chart. Then discuss.

• Hand out any agency codes of practice that apply to your work and discuss.

• Obtain copies of the BAC codes of ethics and practice, and any others that may apply to your work. Discuss.

Learning Points:

• Adherance to personal ethics and values will be the basis for trainees' appreciation of the importance of professional ethics.

• Do not skip this part of training. BAC will advise on how to obtain multiple copies of their codes. It may be worth suggesting or even insisting that agency workers become individual members of BAC. They will then be bound by the codes.

• Do you require telephone workers to sign anything committing them to ethical practice?

My own definition is:

Counselling skills are interpersonal communication skills
derived from the study of therapeutic change in human beings,
used in a manner consistent with the goals and values of the
established ethics of the profession of the practitioner in
question. In addition, the user of counselling skills will find
that their own professional skills are enhanced by the process.

This would then allow teachers, clergy, youth workers, nurses, doctors, managers, educational psychologists, doctors, army officers and many others to use counselling skills in a context-appropriate way. Many professions have codes of ethics and practice (some statutory) which, whilst they do not preclude the use of counselling skills, have elements which may be at variance with counselling values and ethics, e.g. a registered nurse who is technically never 'off-duty' and is sworn to always save life. This means that if the nurse suspects that a person may be in danger from self-harm they are obliged to act, even if this means breaking confidentiality. A counsellor is not bound in this way.

In an attempt to conform to two different sets of values and codes of ethics, many competent helping practitioners are terminally de-skilled by role-conflict. The problem is avoided if the practitioner can feel securely labelled either as a '*counsellor*' or as a 'nurse/teacher/priest *using counselling skills*'. Nurses using counselling skills are bound by their nursing code of practice, whether they are using some counselling skills or not.

As far as the counselling/therapy profession is concerned, there are several professional bodies representing therapists with various theoretical approaches, all of which have their own codes of ethics and practice. The BAC code covers such issues as responsibility to the client and to the wider community, counsellor competence, confidentiality and advertising practice. Copies of both BAC Codes can be obtained from BAC at the address given in the Appendix.

Telephone counselling
On the telephone, as with any mode of helping, we need to decide whether we are 'telephone *counsellors*' or '*using counselling skills* on the telephone'. In this book I am hoping to do two things: firstly, to concentrate upon how to improve our use of counselling skills on the telephone. (This then includes any telephone helping activity e.g. listening, advising, information giving, etc.) Secondly, to acknowledge the growing awareness that real counselling is possible on the telephone. The rest of this chapter summarises the issues surrounding counselling vs using counselling skills on the phone, whilst Chapter 3 looks at bona-fide telephone counselling in more detail.

Before trying to define telephone counselling, many people seem to think that the first question to answer is not "What is it?", but "Can it be done?" (In general, professional bodies such as BAC have been more interested in this latter question - more of this later in this chapter.) In order to answer this question we need to discover whether there is anything implicit in the definitions of counselling which requires that counselling be done face-to-face. For my part I have never found anything that suggests that there is any just cause or impediment to stop *'telephone'* and *'counselling'* being joined in holy matrimony. (The trouble is, no-one has, until very recently, attempted to provide genuine counselling over the telephone.) This does not mean, however, that the provision of a good counselling relationship over the telephone is easy. Counselling in any setting is difficult, and the telephone counsellor is confronted by an additional set of challenges alongside the usual difficulties of working face-to-face. In summary, the main differences relate to:

    i) the quality of psychological contact between the counsellor and client,

    ii) the effect of the telephone on boundary issues,

    iii) the different emphasis on the implementation of certain counselling skills, and

    iv) the effect of the telephone on the counsellor's ability to discharge their ethical and professional responsibilities, including for example, making a contract.

So, if telephone counselling can be done, is it sufficient to define it as 'Doing counselling on the telephone'? My guess is that this definition is probably not adequate because we are forever prone to falling into the trap of thinking that *'on the telephone'* simply means *'out of sight'*. The telephone changes the relationship dynamics in many more ways than just preventing visual contact. I will look at the work of telephone counsellors in Chapter 3.

Using counselling skills on the telephone

As each activity is successively outlined, those remaining become easier to see and identify. Having tied down the differences between 'counselling' and 'counselling skills' it should be a simple matter to put *'using counselling skills'* and *'working on the telephone'* together.

If the use of counselling skills is not limited to counsellors, then many professionals (nurses, teachers, youth workers etc.) should not only be able to use counselling skills but also offer them in their work over the phone. The kinds of telephone activities which will be improved by counselling skills include listening, information giving, advising, guiding and tutoring. This covers services offered by organisations from Samaritans to the Open University, and activities performed by all kinds of designated workers from telephone receptionists through telephone helpline volunteers to distance-learning tutors.

Unless your job includes deliberately inflicting pain and distress on people, the addition of some counselling skills, in my opinion, never degrades any people-related activity. Counselling skills always improve communication and facilitate clearer mutual respect and understanding.

What kind of context or setting?

If a definition of an activity is not complete without identifying the context or setting in which it is practised, we need to look briefly at the kind of settings in which telephone counselling and/or counselling skills might be offered. This will be determined by the factors outlined above, namely, the people (are they qualified?), the context (does the agency call it counselling?) the codes of ethics (counselling or counselling skills or, often, none), etc.

Firstly there are open-access services not requiring specialist referral:

- Where genuine telephone counselling is offered either as a stand-alone service or in association with a face-to-face service e.g. Open Door, Birmingham.
- Drop-in generic or thematic counselling services where the telephone is the first point of contact or an appointment making device e.g. Relate or some Victim Support services.
- Generic 'listening' services, e.g. Samaritans.
- Thematic information, advice and guidance services either telephone only or in association with a walk-in service e.g. Youth Access agencies or Welfare Rights services.
- Thematic helplines e.g. Childline, Aidsline.

Secondly there is a range of agencies and services operated by the health or social services which mostly require specialist referral - GP, social worker or other professional. Again these may use counselling and/or counselling skills as determined by the details of the service. Such services include:
• Community Health Teams, e.g. Alcohol, Drugs or Mental Health.
• Specialist health-related services, e.g. Genetic Counselling, Amputee Counselling.

Thirdly are the few individuals who offer a telephone counselling service as a specialism. This may be as a supplemental support for face-to-face work with people with a disability for example, or as a telephone-only service in a remote rural location, or as a mode of helping because it is simply preferred by both client and counsellor.

Fourthly comes the now burgeoning commercial field of Employee Assistance Programmes which always have a telephone helping component and sometimes this is bona-fide telephone counselling.

Lastly are the 'others', a catch-all bag in which I would include welfare departments in large firms, Open University tutors, Psychiatric Day-Hospitals, and so on.

In all of these settings, I can think of no group of people whose performance would not be improved by counselling skills, and if they do telephone work, an appreciation of how to use counselling skills on the telephone. This book will speak directly to those whose job it is to deal with people in distress on the telephone. Some sections will be of more use to those people working for an agency, some sections will be more useful for those just starting out on training.

For those who are qualified counsellors working on the telephone, I suspect that the majority are trained only to work face to face. Telephone work is a definite specialism worthy of additional professional preparation. There is little training specifically aimed at providing *counselling* rather than counselling skills on the telephone. This book will have something that will help prepare you for work on the telephone, or improve the skills you have acquired 'on the job'.

3 Telephone Counselling

As I have already suggested, there has been considerable debate in recent years as to whether it is possible to do 'real' counselling over the telephone. The echoes of this debate are heard in many arenas concerning themselves with counselling, from training courses to professional bodies such as the BAC. I don't think it would be too wide of the mark to say that up to around three years ago, virtually no-one was prepared to stand up and say that counselling could be done in any medium other than face-to-face.

In Chapter 1 I argued that this position was maintained partly due to intellectual inertia, i.e. that everyone concerned simply made assumptions about what was, and was not, possible based on received wisdom. I further suggested that another factor was the belief that the telephone was somehow second best in terms of preferred human communication media, i.e. even in 'telephone counselling agencies' the general instruction was to get the client in for face-to-face work as soon as possible without frightening them off. Add to this the persistent mythology that suggests that all interpersonal relationships are different on the 'planet telephone' and we have a deadly combination.

In the past ten years we have seen such rapid and substantial change in communications technology that even the counselling world would have to take notice eventually. Whilst I will devote more time to the issue of technology in the next chapter, there can be no doubt that we have been forced to re-evaluate quite what we think is possible in terms of inter-personal relationships. Perhaps we should call these meetings-at-a-distance, that have recently been made more effortlessly possible, 'tele-relationships'. Whatever vocabulary we develop, it is clear that more and more human relationships are being conducted partially or exclusively at a distance, united by various bits of technology from videophones through to computers. We can no longer ignore the suggestion that full-blown, bona-fide, therapeutic counselling is possible at a distance, on the telephone. In accepting this, we have to reconsider our position regarding skills, professional and ethical practice, and maybe even theory.

When it comes to pushing forward the frontiers of tele-counselling, we find forces as diverse as providing accessible services to people with restricted mobility on the one hand, and commercial interests on the other. Whilst there are probably other examples of telephone counselling, I will look at three settings in which I know telephone counselling is practised and in which some effort has been applied to understanding the issues and working with them.

Employee Assistance Programmes

Employee Assistance Programmes or EAPs are commercial operations which offer a range of support services to company employees. The support services are the sort of things that personnel departments used to provide under the banner 'welfare', but are now 'out-sourced' in management jargon which means they are provided by a specialist company. These specialist companies (EAPs) rarely provide on-site support unless there is a 'critical incident', e.g. an industrial accident. EAPs provide a range of services from legal information and support through to full therapeutic counselling. Most of these services are accessed and delivered through the telephone.

For the purposes of this illustration, I am not concerned with the more run-of-the-mill telephone assistance and advice lines, essential to the helping mix though they are, but rather the specialist telephone counselling offered by EAPs as one of their services. EAPs have been working at improving the delivery of support services at distance for around 5 years now and in some cases represent the leading edge of telephone counselling work in the non-voluntary sector. It is interesting to note that the energy behind the development of telephone counselling in this commercial setting is generated by the need to deliver a 'quality' service at the 'right price'.

Telephone counselling helplines

Some specialist helplines have been developed to deliver a range of services, including genuine counselling to users with mobility problems, such as amputees, MS sufferers etc. Such telephone services are often staffed by peer-professionals, i.e. amputees with counselling qualifications counselling amputee callers.

Such services may include a helpline for support and information and, in addition, a dedicated counselling service where the caller is allocated a telephone counsellor who stays with them through an identified counselling relationship, conducted exclusively on the telephone. The counselling relationship may be conducted on an appointments basis, possibly helped by the increasingly sophisticated call management services available on digital exchanges.

Telephone counselling as a supplement to face-to-face work

Some face-to-face counsellors are beginning to use the telephone to supplement their counselling practice in increasingly creative ways. When clients are ill, temporarily immobilised due to injury, at distance due to work, holidays or hospitalisation, counsellors have discovered that the telephone is a more than adequate medium to deliver a counselling session. Also, if a client is in great need or crisis, there is no reason why sessions cannot be scheduled by phone.

Clients with mobility problems can access good quality genuine counselling via the telephone, with some counsellors offering bookable appointment times for telephone counselling sessions. As a supplement to face-to-face work, the telephone extends the range of an individual counsellor's practice and improves accessibility for clients.

Common issues arising in telephone counselling practice

Although the details of practice vary between the different providers of EAPs, specialist telephone counselling helplines and using the telephone as a supplement, a number of issues have emerged as requiring special attention in the delivery of telephone counselling. The following list cannot be exhaustive, since as I hope I have made clear, bona fide telephone counselling is in such a state of rapid development that any snapshot taken today will be out of date tomorrow. Not on the list, but surely on the horizon, is the recognition of telephone counselling by professional bodies such as BAC in terms of knowledge base and competence via Accreditation and in terms of training via Courses Recognition. Of current interest are:

- Qualifications and training for telephone counsellors.
- Working environment of telephone counsellors.
- Conditions of service for telephone counsellors.
- Support and supervision of telephone counsellors.
- Assessment of the caller's current state and needs.
- Contracting; including time limits and confidentiality.
- Boundaries; of the helping relationship, e.g. in EAP work, set by employer's requirements rather than client's needs.
- Referral; within the organisation and/or on to other helping service providers.

It is clear that these are all legitimate concerns of counsellors in general, not necessarily telephone counsellors in particular. The continuing questions are, 'How do we meet these issues on the telephone?' And, 'Are different skills needed for telephone work?'

Qualifications and training for telephone counsellors
When building a team of telephone counsellors, we have exactly the same problems to face that any agency has, namely that of trying to develop recruitment and selection criteria in the absence of any UK qualifications specifically in telephone counselling. EAPs and specialist services have to select on the basis of good face-to-face training, plus the aptitude for, leaning towards, or interest in telephone work. This means that new recruits have not only to be inducted into organisational procedures and policy, but also to receive telephone counselling training, which can be very rudimentary in some cases.

When considering what qualifications the individual counsellor might require before attempting serious telephone work, it is important to realise that special effort will have to be made. The first step in acquiring the skills to make the transition between face-to-face work and telephone counselling is to improve your 'telephone awareness'.

Much of this book is dedicated to developing 'telephone awareness' and it is often assumed that a period of telephone awareness training as a supplement to a diploma in counselling will suffice. The difficulty with this assumption is that the practice of telephone counselling, skills, theory and personal development is never properly integrated and continues to be treated as a bolt-on to face-to-face work. Until new qualifications and training paths dedicated to telephone work are developed, this unsatisfactory situation will prevail. It may be that face-to-face skills and theory are not generic after all, but we will never find out if we don't ask the question and instead continue to assume the answer.

Working environment for telephone counsellors
It has been difficult for those responsible for the development of genuine telephone counselling to break free from the influence of models developed by the voluntary sector. So far, two general ways of structuring the working environment have evolved and are represented in telephone work:

> *A. The first is the development of a **central location** with several telephone counsellors working a variety of shift patterns to cover the advertised hours.*

> *B. The second is where calls are **diverted to counsellors' homes** from a central location, or where the individual counsellor works from home. Whichever method is used, the same issues require consideration:*

• Ergonomics, affecting the physical comfort and mental alertness of the counsellor. E.g. are headsets used or does the counsellor have to hold a handset to their ear for an hour?

> *A*. Easier to control the ergonomics and meet counsellors' needs by central purchasing. A few well equipped workstations will serve many counsellors throughout the week.

> *B*. Difficult to control the ergonomics at a counsellor's home, since it may be difficult to insist on certain requirements or expensive to provide equipment for many counsellors individually.

• Ambient noise, known by psychologists to be a stressor, is best reduced for both counsellor and caller, since hearing background noise can be unnerving for a client.

A. In a busy office environment, ambient noise is quite high. Office machines, air conditioning, chatter and the noise from other telephone conversations can intrude on calls. It is possible to control this, though.

B. Ambient noise at home is likely to be less, if a room is put aside for counselling work. Telephone counsellors using home as a work base will need to reduce the incidence of dogs barking and children being children. These 'home' noises may lead the caller to think that they are intruding, or make them feel more lonely, etc.

• Distractions, no face-to-face counsellor would work in a distracting environment, why should we compromise good practice on the telephone?

A. Again, possibly easier to control in an office situation, but this has to be worked at, not just assumed.

B. Helped by dedicating a room to telephone work and letting the rest of the family know when you are working.

• Information technology support, particularly relevant to agency workers who have computers to hold and retrieve information on, or for, clients as the call is happening.

A. EAPs in particular have good information technology aids for counsellors. Computers active during the call mean that files can be called up giving clients' details, referral routes within the organisation, information regarding other services, etc. will all be available without the counsellor having to move from their seat.

B. Of less relevance to home workers, but there is nothing (save time, effort and cost) preventing individual counsellors or agencies setting up a system to perform the same functions.

• Call monitoring, for ongoing training or routine service evaluation; either by a third person or tape recorder.

A. Used by some agencies as a training or on-going evaluation method. The idea is both to keep telephone counsellors on their toes (you never know when someone is listening) and to give feedback for skills development. The ethics of this are questionable, since agencies may not inform callers that their call is being recorded or listened in to. Sometimes a disclaimer appears in publicity, but this doesn't go far enough in terms of civil liberties.

B. There is nothing to stop individual counsellors from recording telephone conversations at home in order to improve skills; the technology is readily available. But the same ethical problems pertain.

• Backup, supervision and support.

A. Providing telephone counsellors with the necessarily higher levels of backup, support and supervision compared with face-to-face work is easier to achieve in a central location. Staff dedicated to support functions can work on-site in a supervisor or day-leader role, dealing with shift handovers, briefing and debriefings as well as counsellors recovering from a distressing or difficult call.

B. At home a counsellor is usually on their own. The best form of support available will be telephone support. Some agencies arrange this by having shift supervisors or day leaders on call. This form of support is at least congruent with the medium.

Conditions of service for telephone counsellors

This sub-title sounds more like an extract from a trade union manual, and I'm quite happy with that since there really is an issue regarding protecting the rights and working conditions of telephone counsellors, whether paid or voluntary. This is an issue of concern not only for the counsellors themselves but also for their clients. EAPs, for example, will often visit the consulting rooms of their 'counsellors in the field' to ascertain the quality of the environment, whilst paying less attention to the conditions under which their telephone counsellors work. Also, levels of pay expressed as an hourly rate are sometimes not equivalent (with telephone work attracting an inferior rate). This is all the more interesting since I would argue that there is sufficient evidence to demonstrate that telephone counselling is more difficult, requiring more training and more support than face-to-face work, when compared like-with-like.

Conditions worth looking at are:

• Pay; perhaps remuneration for telephone counselling work should reflect the 'counselling' element of the work, rather than the 'telephone' element of the work, since in some cases telephone counsellors are not paid the same rates as face-to-face workers.

Their pay scales are more like souped-up telephone receptionists than therapists.

- Shift patterns; deciding upon working patterns for telephone counsellors would again reflect the 'counselling' element of the work in addition to the 'telephone' element. Taking this as a starting point it might be helpful to ask whether it would be reasonable to expect face-to-face counsellors to work any proposed shift patterns and still be in the right professional and ethical territory.

- Working hours including breaks; as above, would face-to-face counsellors work for three hours at a time without any breaks between clients? Would it be ethical to take call after call without time for restoration, reflection or making notes? It cannot be long before professional bodies address the issue of ethical workloads for telephone counsellors.

- Extra duties; some agencies have working arrangements where anyone not actively occupied picks up other jobs, making tea, filing, even cleaning. Depending upon the nature of the agency, e.g. voluntary sector, this will be more or less acceptable. Some telephone counsellors are the first point of contact in an agency and can be expected to receive all calls, counselling or otherwise. This is more stressful than concentrating upon a sole activity of counselling.

- Support re. sickness and absence; it is acceptable, indeed the epitome of professional practice, to withdraw from client contact under the direction of a supervisor. Sickness and absence procedures will need to acknowledge this in a way that is not punitive. This is no different from face-to-face work, but it is worth reinforcing the point that a telephone counsellor also needs to take time off for more reasons than simply having a bout of the 'flu.

Support and supervision of telephone counsellors
Chapter 9, although dedicated to the general topic of support and supervision, is really aimed at a more general level of helping and listening. Some of the issues regarding telephone counselling are covered there, but here I will concentrate on the specific needs of telephone *counsellors*. This is because, as I have stated elsewhere in this book, much of the custom and practice regarding telephone

work, support and supervision included, has grown up with the under-resourced voluntary sector. Under-resourcing and the fact that much of the work of the voluntary sector is not genuine counselling but listening, advice and guidance or the use of counselling skills, has distorted the nature of the support that telephone workers are likely to be offered.

In Chapters 8 & 9, the following types of support are identified as at least recommended, if not necessary, in telephone helping work. It follows, then that telephone *counsellors* should enjoy similar if not enhanced types and levels of support:
Briefing
On-line support
Debriefing
Supervision
Continuing professional development

The last two types of support are the ones which are likely to separate telephone counsellors from more general telephone listeners and helpers. I suggest that telephone counsellors could start with the face-to-face model of supervision and professional development required by the British Association for Counselling. This model suggests that in order to maintain professional status, a counsellor should receive supervision at the rate of *at least* 1.5 hours per month, dependent upon experience, i.e. the more experienced the counsellor the less supervision required. Experience would suggest that beginning counsellors could work with a ratio of around 1 supervision session per 10 client hours and an experience counsellor could work with a ratio of around 1 supervision session per 25 client hours. Further evidence of professional practice would be to be seen to be meeting these requirements with ease, rather than aiming for the minima.

Telephone counsellors employed by an organisation, or giving their time without charge to a voluntary agency, will find themselves in a similar position to face-to-face counsellors with the exception that there are no specific telephone counselling requirements which can be used to persuade a recalcitrant employer or agency with their eye on the purse strings. When defending the necessity of proper support for telephone counselling, do not compromise your standards of practice, and remember that you can lobby your professional organisation for support in your endeavour to develop and maintain standards.

Assessment of the caller's current state and needs.
Assessment is one of those words that means very different things to counsellors of different persuasions. Some therapeutic approaches make much of a visible, formal assessment process though others, whilst accepting that the process happens at some level, view it as an implicit part of relationship-building.

Notwithstanding these differences, assessment applies to telephone counselling at least as much as it does to face-to-face work. In EAP work, for example, assessment would even include finding out what services the caller is entitled to, depending upon the nature of their employer's contract with the EAP provider (see below). The commercial sector, with a steady eye on efficiency, is also interested in getting the caller to the right helper as quickly and sensitively as possible. Identifying the need for specialist treatment and rapid referral on is a key part of assessment.

Many providers of telephone counselling will also be interested in the kind of assessment performed in acute psychiatry, namely estimating the client's potential for self harm, suicide and doing harm to others. Chapter 7 looks briefly at suicide prevention on the telephone and I would suggest that existing techniques used to assess self and other harm would be adaptable to telephone counselling work. It is worth remembering here that telephone counsellors are unlikely to be dealing with anonymous clients, but may occasionally be faced with a call from a known client from an unknown location, making intervention difficult, should intervention have been contracted for. Chapter 4 looks at telecommunications technology and the possibilities for tracing the location of the caller.

Whatever approach to assessment of the client's needs is adopted, the products of this process will lead on to making some kind of contract with the caller. Assessment and contracting are inextricably linked, not least of all at the level of action required from the counsellor. Face-to-face workers are not expected to be very proactive in maintaining the relationship unless they are making home visits. Telephone counsellors on the other hand will have to build the 'who calls whom' into the assessment and contracting in a deliberate and concrete way.

Contracting; including time limits and confidentiality.
This is the area of telephone work that would appear at first glance to require most thought. I would agree, and at the same time refer readers to my 'Most Useful Question' for assistance. The medium of telephone communication and the 'at distance' nature of the relationship together create a new set of requirements. The notion of a contract in face-to-face work is a sound enough starting point, then telephone counsellors should thoroughly think through the implications of the medium.

Setting time limits on telephone calls is, in one sense, easy enough, yet is somewhat counter to the telephone culture, wherein social calls are thought to be limited by some organic relationship management process and business calls limited by the needs of the working world to get a job done efficiently. Counselling relationships must draw on both telephone cultures to create a safe approach to negotiating time limits for sessions. Voluntary sector telephone services may not be an appropriate model here, since the model which dominates telephone helping culture has at its heart the idea that, 'we never put the phone down on our clients'. Telephone counsellors must define a new telephone culture taking as its foundation the therapeutic requirements of counselling and adapting them without compromise to the telephone medium. This book outlines many of the adaptations necessary in other chapters.

Boundaries; of the helping relationship, e.g. in EAP work, set by employer's requirements rather than client's needs.
The boundaries of a counselling relationship are key to creating the safe space in which clients can work, whether face-to-face or at distance on the telephone. Attention to the way the telephone medium affects boundary setting in assessment and contracting

leads us to the point of deciding if there are any special boundaries that particularly relate to telephone work.

In this regard, the commercial influences on EAP work have determined boundaries such as a limited number of sessions, access to specific services and confidentiality limits. When an employer buys EAP services, they are buying a package of support services based jointly upon what they imagine their employees needs to be and the needs of the employer to have an efficient effective workforce. This will mean that the contract negotiated with the EAP provider will be a set of compromises. Some of these compromises have a direct bearing upon boundaries, contracting and assessment. One example should suffice:

> *Imagine a national road haulage company negotiates an EAP package for all its employees, from maintenance operatives and drivers through supervisors, middle managers to senior management. It considers it necessary to have telephone counselling as the main and primary delivery route, with referral to face-to-face counsellors only for managers above a particular grade. In addition, it wants its drivers and supervisors to have access to a 24 hour legal helpline. Further, it wants a special report to management on every driver who presents with, or is suspected of having, a drug, substance or alcohol related problem.*

How would you configure a telephone counselling service to meet these needs? It is clear that there is a mixture of professional and ethical issues to address before the telephone counsellors on duty know how to respond to a call from an employee of the company in question. Assessment, making a therapy contract and even the therapeutic method may be determined by the boundaries negotiated with the employer.

Although the example above is taken from the commercial sector, the same issues do arise in other settings in modified forms. We cannot assume that counselling on the telephone is a sort of mirror-image of face-to-face work. Individual counsellors using the telephone to supplement their existing face-to-face practice will have to negotiate new telephone boundaries with clients who are ill or temporarily immobile and who may request telephone counselling. Access to your telephone number, who calls whom and what different levels of confidentiality or commitment might be necessary, will all have to be considered.

Referral; within the organisation and/or on to other helping service providers.

Referral skills for telephone counselling are similar to referral skills for face-to-face work. Counsellors will have to consider making an early referral if they realise that the caller's needs fall outside the limits of the agency or their own expertise. Agency policy will probably not allow access to certain clients and in other cases, individual counsellors will find that they are not supported if they choose to work beyond agency limits.

Steve Williams (1993) identifies the following reasons for making a face-to-face referral and this way of looking at referrals provides a helpful framework for telephone workers also:

Reasons for referral (Williams 1993)

Because of you
- Your personal limits
- Your professional limits
- The limits of your competence

Because of the client
- The client needs a wider package of care involving counselling
- The client needs another kind of counsellor
- The client needs other kinds of care (not counselling)

Because of your agency
- Time limits
- Types of service offered
- Policies

Steve Williams then proceeds to outline the management of the referral process, developing a framework for referrals which includes knowing when not to refer, preparing yourself, your client and professional liaison. It is clear that all of these stages of a referral process are relevant to telephone counselling, whether the counsellor wishes to make a referral to another counsellor or service, helper, etc. outside or within the agency itself. A properly qualified counsellor will have well developed referral skills and have a referral network within which they can confidently pass their clients on to trusted helpers and services.

When face-to-face counsellors pass their clients on through referrals, there is always a sense in which they have to let go of their connections with the client. This is also true of telephone counselling, although there is no reason why telephone counsellors should not follow up referrals to see how their client has fared, if this is contracted with the client and is within the model espoused by the counsellor.

Conclusion

Telephone counselling is done by an increasing number of practitioners with a variety of qualifications and experience. Whilst some of the professional issues arising from telephone work require further development by practitioners active in this field, no-one who is qualified to be a counsellor should expect to be any less therapeutic on the telephone than face-to-face.

4 The Impact of Technology

It is difficult, if not impossible, to write anything sensible about technological innovation in communications that will not be out of date by the time this book is published. I could avoid being paralysed by future shock by simply saying that there's nothing that can be done about this ever-changing scenario, simply highlight the problem and leave the rest up to you. I will, however, try to take a snapshot of the current situation, pointing out the implications of changes as we go.

The message of this chapter is that no-one using the telephone to deliver helping relationships can afford to be either complacent or indifferent to technology. If they haven't arrived yet, changes are on the way and you will need to keep abreast.

Technology has not only affected routine telephone communications but the whole range of tele-communications media. Many of the services currently available via the telephone will arrive in our homes in multi-purpose cables delivering television channels, on-line computer communication services such as the much-publicised Internet, video-phones and tele-conferencing, home shopping and tele-banking. I could go on to invent a few more, but I'm sure that my imagination will be outstripped by real life by the time the third edition of this book is available, which will probably be an interactive multimedia programme available on CD-ROM and the Internet!

However, at present, we still need to grapple with the more pressing implications of answer-phones, caller identification, call diversion and itemised billing. Each of the above presents agencies and individuals offering telephone counselling and associated services with issues which need to be resolved immediately. Some have implications for individual practice and some for agency policy.

Answer-phones

Nowadays it may seem that answer-phones are decidedly 'low-tech'. Nevertheless we need to consider the impact of using answer-phones on people that call us for help. If your agency cannot offer a twenty-four hour a day, seven days a week service, there remains the problem of what to do outside of your usual helpline hours. Do you use an answer-phone to carry a message stating your opening times in a reassuring tone? Do you use an answer-phone offering to take messages in addition to your opening times? Do you have no answer-phone at all, leaving the call unanswered?

Issues to consider

There is, of course, no 'correct' answer to this dilemma. Everyone knows that answer-phones have entered into our culture as the things everyone hates to leave messages on. Other folk I know have a policy of never listening to the messages left on their answer-phones (or so they claim). So what are we to make of them?

Best practice?

Whatever we do ourselves when confronted by answer-phones, we must put ourselves in the shoes of our potential callers and clients. How would they feel about hearing an answer-phone message? Is it reasonable to ask callers to leave a message?

• If you are seriously considering using an answer-phone, do make sure you have thought it through by discussing it with your telephone workers.

• You could consider asking callers what they think of the idea.

Caller identification - display and call return

Recently arrived on your phone (if you are connected to a digital exchange) is a facility which will identify the number which is calling you, or has just called you, or the last few numbers that have called you, depending upon the services available and the equipment you have installed. At its most sophisticated you could have a small box (or a phone that has this facility built-in) which will display the number calling you as the phone is ringing (i.e. before you have picked it up), this is called *Caller Display*. Such a box will also display the last number to have called you, even if you did not answer (if you don't have an answer-phone). It will also display the last, say, 10 numbers that you called (whether answered or unanswered) if 1471 is dialed on BT phones; this is known as *Call Return*.

Issues to consider
The problem with this facility is that it allows the receiver of the call to effectively 'trace' calls to the phone at which the call is being made. The intention is to give the receiver the choice of taking calls or not, by knowing in advance the origin of the call. So, when the phone rings and you see that the call is coming from your bank, you could decide, given your current cash-flow, whether you wish to talk to them or not.

In terms of helpline operations or telephone counselling, it may be necessary to reassure callers and potential callers that such technology is not installed or used, thus protecting their anonymity or location (remember caller identification tells you the number, and therefore *where*, the call is calling from). When I say *necessary* I mean that you will have to consider the impact of your position regarding this and other technology upon your potential callers. You will not, under ordinary circumstances, know how many people have been put off calling you because you have failed to give them the assurance of anonymity that they need. The question is can you afford not to reassure them in this way?

You may wish to be of further service to callers by helping to educate them regarding the traps set by this technology and how to avoid them. This might be particularly important for those callers who may be unfamiliar with new telephone services or just plain baffled or frightened by it all, such as children or older people. It is possible to withhold your number from identification by these machines, by pre-dialling a code (141 in the case of BT phones).

Many callers will use payphones and most can be traced with caller display equipment or by using call return. Payphone numbers can also be withheld using 141. It may reassure your clients if they know this. Some helplines have the policy of calling clients back, either to save them money, or perhaps with information, or maybe to check that they are OK. It may be important to block your number with 141 before doing this so that if someone other than your client is there, they cannot trace the call to your helpline. In the case of children, women and others vulnerable to abuse, this may be a matter of life or death. For others it will prevent their friends and relativesknowing that they have contacted or are being contacted by a helpline.

Best practice?
It is important that those calling helplines and telephone counsellors feel assured that their interests are being *actively* looked after in terms of confidentiality and protection of their identity. Ignorance of the power of new technology does leave some service users vulnerable to identification.
  • Tell callers the consequences of caller identification technology, how to block it by withholding numbers using 141 and your agency policy on tracing numbers using caller display equipment.
  • Use your discretion when introducing this information into calls; you could include some information in your publicity.

Call diversion
This facility is available free and automatically to some subscribers and by monthly charge to others, depending upon the telephone company. By dialling in a special code, subscribers are able to divert incoming calls to any other number they choose, either directly with no delay or on 'no answer'.

Some helplines use call diversion to operate a service from a 'dummy number'. What happens is the caller will be diverted, often without their knowledge, to the phone of the person on duty that day. The caller will have dialled one number, but will be put through to another phone, usually at the home of the duty telephone counsellor.

Issues to consider
There are some advantages to this facility in that the helpline can run without having to maintain expensive premises, or without the necessity for volunteers to travel in to a central office. If a volunteer

is unavailable for any particular reason, the calls can easily be diverted to another volunteer's number who is willing to substitute or swap. Call diversion, whilst not commonplace, is used by some helplines who contend that they could not operate without it. In some geographically remote areas it may indeed make the difference between a helpline or no helpline at all.

There are, however, some disadvantages to using call diversion in helpline work. One minor disadvantage is that some call diversion systems give the caller a message saying 'Please hold, your call is being diverted' or something similar. This message, or any interruption in the call, is enough to put anxious callers off. They may worry that the call is being monitored or that it is being diverted to some unknown destination. The most serious disadvantage is not so much the call diversion process itself, but the use to which it is being put. Although many helplines do it (some out of necessity), it is not good practice to have a dummy number which diverts calls to helpline volunteers' homes. This is explored in greater detail in *'Working environment for telephone counsellors'* on page 27.

Best practice?
Only use call diversion in emergencies or very short periods to tide you over a change in premises.
    • Do everything you can to avoid diverting calls to volunteers' homes, regardless of whether you use dedicated mobile phones or the volunteers' home number.

Itemised billing
Most readers will be familiar with itemised telephone bills and the advantages they bring. Having control over telephone use is vital to many households. Some of the consequences of itemised billing are not so handy if you wish to make private calls undetected, as many chatline-phoning teenagers have found out. Telephoning from work may not help either, since most workplaces have an itemised bill or a call-management system which will identify not only times, dates and numbers dialled, but also the extension from which they are dialled (these details are often printed out weekly or monthly). Such

call-management systems, since they are internal exchange facilities these systems will also log 0800 or Freephone numbers.

On some bills all calls costing over 50 pence are logged, whilst on others all charged calls are itemised for all the world to see. This means that even if a caller asks you to call them back, their call, however brief will appear on a fully itemised bill. Usually, 0800 or Freephone numbers are not logged on domestic itemised bills because the subscriber doesn't pay for them. (The purpose of the itemising is to give detailed accounts of charges.) All other calls to helplines, 'chatlines' or 'sex lines' will show up on the bill, neatly logged with the date, time and cost.

Issues to consider
This means that an account of who we've been speaking to is available to anyone who has sight of our telephone bill and it becomes impossible to have a 'private' or 'discrete' telephone call undetected. For many callers this so compromises their ability to make a helpline call that they simply don't do it and for some this could mean the difference between life and death. Women, children, older and infirm people are all at risk from discovery that they have been calling for help.

Using a BT Chargecard will not conceal the caller's identity since the calls made on the chargecard will appear on the itemised bill of the domestic number to which they relate. Date, time, cost and number dialled will appear under 'chargecard calls'.

An abused child or woman is at risk for at least two reasons, firstly, as I mentioned above, they may not make the call that would start the process of preventing the abuse, knowing that the call would appear on their family's bill. Secondly, they may innocently make a call for help, not appreciating that it would subsequently appear on the bill. This could lead to horrific retribution should the perpetrator find out.

Best Practice?
Again good practice would suggest that you take an active role in letting your callers know the possible dangers of using your service.

Tell them how best to avoid detection via itemised bills or call-management systems.

• If there is a real risk, they should not use their home phone, work phone, or indeed any phone where someone, whom they do not feel is 'safe', will see the bill . It is best to use:

• A public payphone (this can be inconvenient or sometimes impossible, and may be neither private nor confidential - see page 61).

• A 'safe' phone e.g. belonging to a friend or relative that can be relied upon and trusted.

• If possible include some of this information in your agency publicity.

Last number re-dial

The majority of telephones are fitted with a 'last number re-dial' button which does just that - re-dial the last number dialled. It is a great labour-saving device when the number you dial is engaged.

Issues to consider

Small conveniences can turn out to be curses for helpline users. Most telephone users who want to cover their tracks (teenagers, for example) have worked out that anyone can find out who you called last by pressing the re-dial button and seeing who answers. This can be covered by dialling a 'safe' or 'neutral' number after any number you wish to conceal.

Best practice?

Yet another case of letting your service users know how to protect themselves against detection. Such help may be particularly important for children or housebound women.

• Tell your callers the dangers of last number re-dial and how to cancel them out.

• This doesn't get around the problems of itemised billing, however, so separate action will need to be taken by those callers who are particularly at risk.

In Training: It is important to sensitise trainees to the technological issues to help them become 'technology-aware'. The safety of callers should be high up on the list of priorities for telephone counsellors.

Method:

• Introduce trainees to technology issues and invite discussion of the best ways of informing callers of the dangers.

• Try developing a vignette or two where a caller presents a technological dilemma appropriate to your service, e.g. a child or woman in danger, or a person with mobility problems who doesn't want their family to know they're calling a helpline.

Learning Points:

• Agency publicity should be clear and informative where technology is concerned. Ask workers to help in formulating publicity and ask callers to evaluate it, if at all possible.

• Agency policy should have a section on technology and the agency rules regarding best practice in certain situations.

5 Before the Call

Getting ready to start telephone counselling is rather like going on holiday or making a long car journey - careful preparation makes all the difference between a successful event and possible disaster. You would not think of making a long car journey without :
- planning your journey; route, stops, etc.
- checking the mechanical condition of the car,
- filling up with petrol, water and oil,
- making sure you have enough qualified drivers,
- correct insurance and
- a map.

Good practice in counselling requires us to have a similar sort of pre-counselling checklist. Having such a checklist for counselling is, in essence, no different whether we are counselling on the telephone or face-to-face, but our pre-counselling checklist will be somewhat different in each circumstance. For telephone work, my checklist is divided into two sections:

i) The agency checklist (things an agency must do to provide an effective service and to protect its workers/volunteers and clients).

ii) The individual counsellor's checklist (things you and I must do as counsellors to ensure we and our clients are safe, enabling us to work to our full potential).

Very few people do telephone counselling on their own, although this small number may increase. Most people belong to some telephone counselling organisation either as a paid worker or unpaid volunteer. The agency you work for should come up to your standards of professional practice just as much as you need to come up to theirs. *(Note: You should not compromise on your standards if you are a volunteer. Make your requirements known and stick to them if you value the quality of your work - paid or voluntary.)*

For your own protection and the safety of your clients, think hard about working in an agency which does not provide the basic facilities and services on the checklist. If the agency does not have a policy, do not despair. With other responsible members you could help the agency develop a policy appropriate to the needs of the workers and the client group. Would you travel in a car without a current MOT, or with an unqualified driver without insurance?

Agency Checklist:

Agency Policy - is there one?

If Yes does it cover:
•Training
•Support and supervision

•Boundaries
•Advertising
•Worker/volunteer personal safety
•Equal opportunities for
  workers & clients
•Legal issues
•Insurance
•Abusive calls

•Referrals

•Silent calls

*Are there enough workers/
volunteers?*
Does the rota system work?
Are the premises adequate?
*Is the telephone system
adequate and appropriate
for the service?*
For how long is funding secure?

Personal Checklist:

*Do you feel properly
supported on the following
issues by the agency:*
•Sufficient training
•Adequate support &
  supervision
•Boundaries
•Congruent advertising
•Your personal safety
•Countering discrimination

•Understanding the law
•Are you insured?
•Do you have to listen to
  abuse? Are you allowed to
  put the phone down on
  abusive callers?
•Who do you take referrals
  from and make them to?
•Are you allowed to end
  silent calls?

*Do you feel personally able
to take on this work today?*
Have you left your
*Have you left your
personal issues behind*
*Are you familiar with the
agency routines?*

Well, how did you and your agency do? This chapter will be explaining each of the issues in turn and giving some recommendations for good practice where appropriate. Don't worry if you or your agency haven't yet covered all the issues mentioned above; we all have to start somewhere. Only worry if you have identified a shortfall but neither you nor your agency want to do anything about it.

The checklist above may not be exhaustive - this is deliberate since it is imperative that each agency develops policy and procedures that are appropriate for the service it is offering. I'm sure you will be able to add to it and I'm equally sure some agencies will not like having some of these issues raised in this way. I do not apologise for this. Agencies must realise that good practice is neither optional nor a luxury, it is the basis for public helping. If you cannot guarantee safe, effective practice, do not offer anything.

In Training: Good, ethical practice begins long before a client is present, so it is important to introduce the idea of preparing for work with clients early on in training.
Method:
• Introduce the idea of preparing for a journey, then ask trainees to make up their own pre-counselling safety checklists in small groups. Share and discuss in large group.
Learning Points:
• Not only does it highlight issues for trainees, it may well give the agency clues as to how well it meets acceptable standards of practice if it doesn't have a policy yet.

Personal Checklist: Agency Policy

The first question on the Personal Checklist implies that:
    i) there is an agency policy (however adequate) and
    ii) that you know about it and what it says.
Your first task is to find out whether there is one and track down a copy to check it out. Every agency offering counselling, advice or guidance of any description should have a policy covering the issues

on the checklist. I cannot emphasise this strongly enough. A good policy creates a sound structure or framework within which you can safely work with your clients. It is, if you like, the agency's way of creating the **core conditions for** *providing* **counselling** (see Chapter 6) within which you, the counsellor can be effective. You could say that an agency policy covering the points above is **necessary but not sufficient** (see Chapter 6) for an effective service.

An agency without a policy will fail to provide a safe working environment for its counsellors and so, by extension, its clients. If counsellors do not have sound guidelines on confidentiality and referrals, adequate backup, support and supervision, sufficient and appropriate training or work in an agency that doesn't have a clear idea about the work that it does, then they cannot give 100% of their attention to their clients.

For counselling to be successful the counsellor must give full attention to the client, confident in the knowledge that the agency is holding the safety net woven from the elements listed above. Counsellors should do the counselling and the agency should take care of the rest. Let's see how this might work out in practice. Because this book is aimed at individual counsellors, I will tackle the points on the *Personal Checklist* and, where appropriate, make reference to agency policy as I go.

Training and Supervision

If I had to pick two elements which are absolutely essential to the running of any counselling agency, they would be training and supervision. It is no accident, then, that you find them at the top of both the personal and agency checklists. Training and supervision share certain features:

• All professional counsellors acknowledge them as essential requirements for effective, responsible counselling practice.
• They are both required by the British Association for Counselling before we can become Accredited Counsellors.
• Both are ongoing processes. Neither can ever be said to be finished or complete.
• Successful counsellors are not only committed to ongoing

personal and professional development through training and supervision, they positively relish both.

• You should not call what you are doing 'counselling' unless you have a professional counselling qualification and are adequately supervised.

• Agencies should not offer 'counselling' unless the staff are properly trained and adequately supervised.

Supervision will be covered in Chapter 9, and training is covered from a number of angles throughout the book. In Chapter 11 Anna Karczewska describes the training provided by Family Contact Line. Here, I look at some general issues in the training of counsellors and telephone helper/listener/counsellors.

Training - general principles

As a freelance trainer I am often asked to run a weekend session on counselling skills, after which the participants are expected by their employers to demonstrate their new-found proficiency on the poor, unsuspecting public. In a similar vein, people expect to become proficient in counselling after completing a ten 'veek evening class. I mention these examples in particular because many telephone counselling agencies think this is enough. It is not enough. Whilst any training is probably better than none, we must be careful not to overestimate what can be achieved in a short time period and in my experience, some training does prove that the old saying 'a little knowledge is dangerous' can sometimes be true. So how much is enough?

Some readers will already have completed counselling skills training or even counsellor training, whilst many will have undergone a short training course to prepare them for volunteer helpline work. Because much of the training currently available concerns itself with face-to-face work, and both counsellors and counselling skills practitioners are simply expected to make the transition from face-to-face to telephone with the minimum of preparation, I will look at both training for face-to-face helping and training dedicated to telephone work. Wherever possible, seek out specialised telephone training and agencies that offer it.

Face-to-face counselling training

There have been various recommendations regarding the length of training required to equip the average person with sufficient skills to do various types of counselling. Unfortunately, the vast majority of the effort has gone into setting standards for face-to-face counselling in one-to-one relationships. Current thinking suggests that a course needs to have at least 100 hours 'contact' in order to train people to use *counselling skills*. Many college evening classes are around this length - it represents one evening a week for an academic year. A course of over 400 hours 'contact' is recommended to train *counsellors*. Good reference points here are the BAC Courses Recognition Scheme and the BAC Individual counsellor Accreditation Scheme. Both aim to train counsellors, not users of counselling skills. The Courses Recognition Scheme suggests a minimum of 400 hours training contact, excluding supervised practice. In order to be an Accredited Counsellor, you will need a mixture of training and experience which if you follow what is known as the 'qualifications route' requires 450 hours training *plus* 450 hours supervised practice over three years.

If all this sounds a little daunting, remember that *counselling* is a difficult and skilled activity carrying weighty responsibility. Not everyone is suited to counselling, nor will everyone who enters training be successful in gaining the qualifications.

A further question relates to the period of time over which these contact hours should occur. Should they be done in one block or over a certain number of weeks? Here personal and/or agency circumstances will suggest particular patterns. Some people believe that learning counselling takes a while. The changes in attitudes and development of skills required can take some time to 'ferment', like good wine. Certain flavours can't develop overnight; they need a certain amount of ageing. It may be that the best results are obtained when training lets this consolidation of learning take place at a more 'natural' pace, rather than put it in the pressure cooker environment of an intensive training programme. If you are making a big investment in training it may be more important to get the best trainers possible and choose a course timetable that your workers can most comfortably manage.

Lastly, the size of the training group is very important. It is clearly impossible to 'teach' counselling skills to a group of thirty people. The process requires close attention to each group member and good feedback to each individual. How many trainees can a good trainer give such attention to at any one time? Many trainers work in pairs (this is good practice and some accrediting bodies require it), but a trainer-trainee ratio of 1 to 15 for theory and personal development and 1 to 8 for skills is about right. Up to a point, smaller groups are an improvement, larger groups degrade the training experience.

Telephone counselling training
It is difficult, if not impossible, to make any sensible statement about standards in telephone counselling for a number of reasons.
• The whole area of telephone work has grown up in the voluntary sector, traditionally starved of funds and so always trying to get the best value for money, sometimes at the expense of quality.
• If an agency is dependent upon volunteers, it is unreasonable to expect the volunteers to spend months or years in training before being allowed to do the work for which they have volunteered.
• Since the workers are volunteers, it has been difficult for agencies to say 'You're not good enough', when people prove not to be up to scratch.
• No professional body has yet sat down to discuss and set out standards for telephone work, largely for the reasons mentioned in Chapter 1.
• Telephone work has, so far, been fragmented in the UK. No single body has been formed or taken responsibility for this specialised area of work.

There is hope, however, since a number of the blocks to progress outlined above have seen movement in recent months.
• Telephone work has been developed by EAPs in the commercial sector and training is no longer starved of funds.
• Professional bodies are beginning to take an interest (e.g. looking at the possible accreditation of telephone counsellors) and are developing standards (e.g. NVQs in counselling include telephone competencies).

• Moves are being made to bring together telephone helplines to share experiences, model good practice and set standards (e.g. The Telephone Helplines Association, see Appendix p 193).

In general terms, a good counsellor should be 'well rounded'. That is to say that they should:
• have a good grasp of the theory of counselling,
• be able to demonstrate good counselling skills, and
• have a reasonably high degree of self-awareness, gained from personal development.

A further ingredient is that the first three components must be congruent. In other words, the theory, skills and personal work must be in harmony, drawn from the same general approach or if drawn from many sources (eclectic), integrated in a logical, thoughtful and meaningful way. So the training must have a *core theoretical model* such as Person Centred, Psychodynamic, or Cognitive. If the preference is for an integrative approach, then a core theoretical model such as the integrated eclectic approach of Gerard Egan might be appropriate. It is not good practice to have a hotchpotch of bits of approaches bolted together at whim or just because it's what the trainers know from the books they've read.

The above four elements or qualities of a good counsellor must also be represented in training for telephone counselling. Training should have a good balance between theory, skills and personal work, and be congruent. How might these elements be represented in training people to be counsellors or counselling skills practitioners on the telephone?

Theory
In one sense, theory is easy enough to find and incorporate into telephone counselling training, since there are plenty of good books available. It might appear to be a drawback that there is no theory that relates to telephone work specifically, but my argument throughout this book is that we should first ask ourselves whether we *need* to pay any special attention to the medium of communication. There is little in theories of counselling and psychotherapy that suggest they cannot be adapted to working on the telephone. There

are plenty of good books covering a range of theories from introductory level to diploma level and beyond. I have listed some of my favourites in the Appendix on page 193.

However, a good trainer is required in order to help present the theory in an accessible way and so that it can be translated into effective practice. That is where skills training comes in.

Telephone counselling skills

Although the sub-title of this section is *Telephone counselling skills,* we actually find that it is necessary to look at separate sets of skills:
 • Face-to-face counselling skills: those skills which *require* face-to-face contact in order to deliver the active ingredients of the helping relationship.
 • Counselling skills which do not require any particular medium or setting: those which can be practised face-to-face or at distance, whether it be on the telephone, or any other medium.
 • Telephone-specific counselling skills: those skills which are particular to the telephone as a medium of communication.

This book largely concerns itself with this last category of skills. The first task is to identify the skills in each category, so that training can be designed and targeted to meet the learning needs of the trainees. One of the aims of this book is to get you, the reader, thinking in 'telephone-sensitive' ways so that you automatically test skills in your head and put them into one of the above categories.

Learning to do telephone counselling (and counselling in general) can be compared to learning how to drive a car:
 • You need practical experience built in to the learning process. It is not enough to know the theory of driving, you have to practice the skills of driving as well.
 > *Knowing counselling theory is not enough. Counselling is a skills- based activity and cannot be developed just by reading books.*
 • You need to get practical experience in a gradual way, first in the safety of a dual control vehicle under the watchful eye of an approved instructor, moving on to practice in between

lessons with the instructor by going out into the traffic with a friend or relative who has already passed their test.

> *Developing counselling skills is best done in as near to a 'real' counselling setting as possible. Training courses must build in this kind of activity. Role playing is only good enough for very simple exercises. There is no substitute for real counselling.*

• When learning to drive a car you are exposed to almost every type of traffic situation.

> *If possible, training should provide varied experiences of counselling, including opportunities for the development of skills appropriate for ongoing counselling. Some training courses only offer opportunities to practice the initial interview over and over again.*

• You have to have special instruction for each different type of vehicle you are intending to drive, cars, motorcycles, HGVs, etc.

> *Training for face -to-face counselling is not sufficient for working on the telephone. There are separate and different elements of knowledge, skills and self-awareness. It is not possible to simply transfer from one to the other without extra or different training.*

• You have to pass your driving test in order to drive unaccompanied on the roads.

> • *Training without standards, assessment or evaluation is as good as no training at all. Training in counselling, whether for the telephone or not, must pass people 'fit for practice', which means that some people will not make it. Maybe they will need longer to acquire the skills, knowledge and self-awareness, or maybe they are just not suited to this kind of work, however enthusiastic they are. Agencies must bear the responsibility of protecting callers from incompetent practitioners. This can, of course, be a difficult and sensitive area when the agency runs on volunteers.*

This whole area of skills training is covered in Chapter 6, which looks at counselling skills and how they can be put into practice on the telephone but as I have pointed out, I don't believe that reading this book will be enough. That's why it's called **'An Incomplete Guide'**. What's missing is you and your experience, particularly your counselling skills practice. This can only be developed in relationships with others and these training relationships with your peers are the pivot around which your developing counselling skills turn. Not only do these relationships give you a 'safe' arena in which to practise your budding skills, they also give you the opportunity to receive good feedback and finally they give you and your fellow trainees the opportunity to be a client in counselling. (More on this in a moment.) Don't worry if your skills aren't tip-top to begin with, you'll get better and your colleagues will know that in this training relationship you'll be taking risks and using them as 'guinea pigs'. Don't settle for training that *only* offers role-plays.

Training should be a mixture of as wide a range of practical experiences as possible. These experiences should be appropriate for the type of work you are being prepared to do and best practice would include some active telephone experience. By this I mean using real telephones to practise receiving calls. This can be achieved by:
- using specially made training equipment.
- adapting exiting installations where more than one extension is available.
- having an extended period of training to include a 'probation' or trial period on the lines before finally passing trainees fit to practise, and including:
  - Making use of 'pseudo calls', i.e. people acting as stooges (not real clients) posing as real clients phoning the line for trainees or to continue to evaluate experienced workers.
  - Having trainers or supervisors listening in to the call (this can have ethical implications, i.e. do you inform callers, and if so when and how?).

The tape-recording of some of these training calls will permit playback and feedback for more learning.

Personal development

Some think that this is the most important ingredient in training, to the extent that they believe that people become good enough counsellors after an extended period of personal therapy or group work. I don't share that particular view, but I would not recommend any training that didn't make a firm commitment to personal work in some shape or form. Personal development is interesting in that the prospect of it fills some with enthusiastic excitement and others with fear and suspicion. We can map out our developing self-awareness using a *johari window* (see below) in which we can see the functions of training experience:

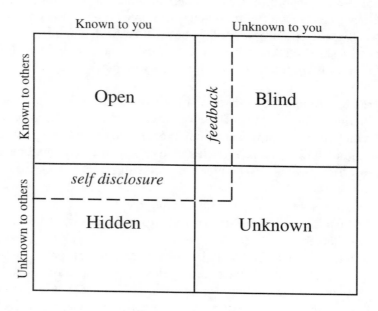

For those unfamiliar with this diagram, the *open* area is your conscious, open behaviour, known to you and others. The *blind* area is where others can see things about you that you cannot see yourself. The *hidden* area represents things we know about ourselves which we do not reveal to others. The *unknown* area includes feelings and motivations within you but unknown to both yourself and others. You know it's there because from time to time some of these aspects of yourself become known, and then you realise that these previously unknown feelings have been influencing your behaviour all along. Those of us that are frightened of personal development work are often afraid of what the unknown and blind areas might hold, or that we may be forced to reveal the contents of the hidden area. In order for personal development to take place in training, we need to see that the learning environment has an appropriate balance of challenge and safety or support.

When I say that telephone counsellors need to be self-aware, I mean that through ongoing self development (including opportunities available in telephone counselling skills training) we seek to expand the 'Open' area in the *johari window*. This is achieved in personal development by two complimentary processes that are facilitated by the trainer in as safe an environment as possible:
    i) receiving *feedback* from others and
    ii) by talking about ourselves honestly as we can, or *self-disclosure*.

Those using counselling skills on the telephone also:
- Need to be sufficiently emotionally stable and self aware to be able to respond well to the emotional content of calls.
- Should not use the service or callers to meet their own emotional or other needs.
- Should be able to work as a member of a team if working in an agency.
- Should know their own skill and emotional limitations.
- Should be open and able to accept feedback and incorporate suggestions into new ways of being and working.
- Should be actively committed to counselling as an acceptable agent for positive change and growth, this includes the idea that they might be a client themselves in order to further their own self-development.

Anyone who will not participate in the personal development activities in a counselling skills training programme cannot be assured of meeting these criteria. In particular, they will not have demonstrated their basic *faith* in the counselling process (the last criterion) since the best evidence of such faith would be for them to submit to the process as a client or participant in self development.

Would you go to a dentist who was afraid to visit the dentist her/ himself or thought that they somehow didn't need to go? Such a dentist would be a poor prospect indeed and I would worry about their sensitivity to my anxieties about dentists and their appreciation of the pain I might feel if they have never been in the dentist's chair themselves.

When asked to participate as a client in a real counselling session in a training situation, I sometimes hear trainees say 'But I haven't got any problems or anything to talk about. I'd rather make something up.' My experience is that everyone has something to talk about - a difficult decision, something mildly upsetting that happened at home or work, something that they saw on television that got to them on an emotional level, and so on. The counselling sessions in training need not be packed with world shattering problems from the depth of your soul and can remain confidential if necessary.

However 'safe' the topic selected for such practice sessions is, great care must be taken to respect the person doing the talking in the client position. Safe, superficial personal issues can suddenly touch upon something deeper which will need all the skills the counsellor can muster. Do not be afraid of these moments, if you do your best to offer the core conditions (See Chapter 6), you will be able to provide a safe space for your colleague to explore their issues. If you find that you are getting beyond your competence or confidence, ask for help from the trainer. This should be good practice for those moments (which are usually few and far between) when we are beyond our limits and need to tell our clients in a caring and responsible way as quickly as possible.

What the telephone means to me
Some readers might be at a loss to know how to focus personal development specifically to use of the telephone. One exercise that I have had some success with, I call *Telephone Baggage.*

The term 'baggage' is often used in counselling circles to mean unhelpful learning from past situations which we bring with us to the present situation. It weighs us down, distorts our movement and generally holds us back from doing what we want, just like carrying around real baggage. The term is used in face-to-face training in association with personal development and it is generally thought that we would be better counsellors if we could identify this extra weight we are carrying around with us and, hopefully, get rid of some or all of it.

In Training: I have found that it can be a good starting point for personal-awareness development if we take a moment to get a new perspective on what the telephone means to us and see if we bring any telephone baggage with us to each call we receive.

Method:

• Begin by introducing the idea that the telephone carries different meanings for each of us, for some it may be the bringer of good news, for others it may be associated with bad news or tragedy. Sometimes the telephone is a lifeline, a link to cherished friends or relatives, for others a curse that reminds them of work or responsibilities every time it rings.

• Ask the group to take a moment or two to reflect on the personal meanings that the telephone holds for them as individuals.

• Share the outcome of this contemplation in twos, each person taking 5 - 10 minutes, with the listener using counselling skills to help the talker explore.

• Bring issues back to the large group to share.

Learning Points:

• The telephone may, for some trainees, be associated with very powerful feelings left over from past events. Do respect everyone's contribution, however apparently 'small'.

• Remind trainees that this is their telephone baggage. Can they leave it behind every time the telephone rings whilst they are on duty, or will they carry it invisibly into each new call?

Boundaries

When I first heard the word 'boundaries', it didn't take long for me to realise that although I hadn't used the word in this context before, I was all too familiar with the concepts. The closest single word that explains 'boundaries' in the world of counselling, is the word 'rules', but counsellors would never use the word '*rules*'! The term 'boundaries' is more figurative than 'rules' since it indicates an enclosed space; sacred space, safe space, open space, the client's space, space in which to grow. In order to give the counselling space these qualities, we need to protect it with boundaries. These boundaries will keep certain worldly things out and certain counselling values in, for example:

Out:	sexual contact	**In**:	empathy
	other exploitation		warmth
	gossip		confidentiality
	hierarchy		genuineness

A good list of boundaries can be found in the BAC Codes of Ethics and Practice. (Although they are not specifically referred to as boundaries in these publications.) There are different Codes for Counsellors, Counselling Skills, Trainers and Supervisors. Your agency should have copies of *all* those available, if not, copies are available from BAC at the address given in the Appendix on p.193.

In Training: The boundaries that are appropriate for telephone work will be different from the boundaries counsellors are familiar with in face-to-face work. It may be helpful to start with the more familiar ground of face-to-face counselling. *Method:*

• Ask small groups of trainees what features they would require in a face-to-face relationship in order to create a safe/secure/sacred space for themselves. Share and discuss.

• Do the same exercise but this time for safe/secure *telephone* relationships.

• Share and discuss, look at the differences.

Learning Points
- How close are the elements generated by trainees to BAC Codes?
- How closely does this match with agency policy?

So what boundary issues are of particular importance in telephone relationships? To some extent this depends upon the agency you work for, since the service it is offering will determine sensible boundaries. Clearly some boundaries will be more important than others. Tick off the important ones for you and your agency in the following list:
- Confidentiality.
- Counsellor anonymity.
- Gifts/payment from clients.
- When should a counsellor not accept a particular caller/client?
- Counselling friends/acquaintances or becoming friends with clients.
- Sexual contact with clients.
- Counselling clients of other helping agencies.
- Is face-to-face contact permitted, prohibited or encouraged?
- Who can end calls - counsellor or client only?

Each issue in the list above needs careful consideration by agencies offering telephone services. We will look at the importance of knowing where your agency stands in relation to each one in the section on Congruent Advertising. For the moment, I will highlight the boundary issue which occurs in all counselling settings and has a slightly different emphasis for telephone work: confidentiality.

'Confidentiality' and 'Privacy' are different.
On the phone it's important to distinguish between these two features of the counselling boundary. This problem would not occur in a face-to-face setting since it would be assumed that the interview was private, i.e. that no-one else is present.

Confidentiality refers to the treatment of information disclosed to you by the client, including their identity.

Privacy refers to the setting in which the counselling takes place. A setting can be somewhere on a sliding scale between private or public.

Some public settings can be confidential - sitting on a park bench with no-one else in hearing range. Some private interviews are not confidential. Privacy is a condition which can be infringed at either end of the phone - the client may be phoning from a public telephone or may have someone else in the room with him/her, and the counsellor may have other counsellors in the same room when the call is being received. Such infringements of privacy are often detectable by both counsellor and client. It is important that the counsellor doesn't make claims for the counselling that can't be guaranteed. Don't say the agency provides a private and confidential service if you can guarantee only one condition or neither.

Privacy

Clients might expect their call to be received in private and confidential surroundings, regardless of what your publicity says. Although I've never seen any agency which says - "All calls are confidential but not private". How would your client feel if after hearing your assurances that the call is confidential, they could hear other voices in the background (a common experience for callers to helplines) or a voice saying, 'Hey, Pete, would you like a cup of coffee?'

At the client's end, privacy could be disturbed by someone coming into the room. This can often be signalled by changes in the client's behaviour such as giving one word answers, hesitations and pauses in mid-sentence, losing track of ideas etc. If this happens, say to your client:

> *'It sounds as if someone has walked in on you. If they have, just answer, 'Yes'.'*

You can then either ride out the intrusion or move to a swift reassuring close using 'Yes'/'No' answers from your client. In some cases a client will just hang up without warning to protect their privacy.

It is important that you feel supported by agency policy and office rules as far as privacy and noisy surroundings are concerned. Agency policy may say:

> Counselling calls **will** be taken in private.
>
> Closed doors **will** be respected.
>
> **No** talking in the office when a call is taken.
>
> Extension phones **must not** be left plugged in.
>
> Eavesdropping is **not** allowed.

Confidentiality
Keeping information disclosed by clients confidential is a major factor in establishing an environment in which your clients can feel safe and secure. In order to avoid confusion amongst agency workers and to protect counsellors, there should be an agency policy on confidentiality. You may even like to consider asking every worker to sign a written statement on confidentiality as part of your recruitment procedure.

Agency policy should be:
- clearly written,
- available to all workers, not just counsellors,
- made known to all callers at appropriate times during their helping relationship,
- fully explained in training and induction to all agency workers.
- preferably developed by, or in partnership with, volunteers/ workers, not 'imposed' by management,
- in a constant state of revision, never 'finished'.

Agency policy should cover:
- The categories of information that are confidential.
- Under what circumstances and to whom confidential information would be disclosed.
- Lines of support in confidentiality disputes.
- Who has the final say in matters of disclosure of information - client, counsellor, supervisor, manager?
- The legal position on confidential records.

Examples of agency statements on confidentiality:
- Confidentiality is not kept just between the individual worker and client. Confidentiality is shared between past, present and future workers.
- Do not speak about callers when off duty, even when you think the caller cannot be identified.
- Only talk about callers to other agency workers when on duty, always protect their identity. Always have a reason to talk about a caller (e.g. supervision or support), never gossip.
- Never break confidence without the client's knowledge.
- Always seek the client's permission before speaking to a third party.
- Only the agency manager may speak to anyone outside the agency e.g. police, social services, GP's etc.

The legal position

As far as the legal situation is concerned, the law is constantly changing in two respects. Firstly, the various laws concerning confidential information are occasionally re-written. And secondly, as cases are tried in Court, certain judgements set legal precedents. Therefore, anything written here, today, may well be out of date by the time you read it. Agencies should seek legal advice before writing their policy on confidentiality to ensure maximum protection for both their staff and their clients.

In general, agencies and individuals do not have to disclose information to the police or anyone else for that matter (there are two exceptions - see below) even when the information concerns crimes as serious as murder. You will not commit an offence by withholding information asked for unless,

> i) it relates to the Prevention of Terrorism Act, when withholding information without reasonable excuse is an offence, and
> ii) you are ordered by a court to produce information and you refuse, in which case you may be in contempt of court and may be fined or imprisoned.

For further information get hold of a copy of the leaflet 'Counselling, Confidentiality and the Law', published by BAC (see p.193). If you ever tangle with the law, seek legal advice immediately and don't give any information unless advised to do so. Even then it's up to you. Your legal adviser will tell you the probable consequences of withholding information. However you are unlikely ever to be in the position where confidentiality and your ethical position brush anywhere near the law, but it is essential that you and your agency are prepared.

Some agencies may keep information on a computer. Whether this is information on clients, staff, sponsors or any other individuals, you may have to register under the Data Protection Act. Again, seek advice from a legal expert or the Data Protection Act Registrar's office.

Advertising

The purpose of advertising is to let potential clients or service users know that you are offering telephone helping/listening or counselling. It is important that your advertising material is thoughtfully prepared and placed. It should be:

- Accurate; don't advertise services that you don't provide.
- Informative; remember to give all relevant opening times and contact numbers.
- Ethical; don't advertise services that you are not qualified to offer, or claim that you can do things that you are not able to.
- Targeted; to your client group.
- Promoting equality of access, if appropriate; this may be modified if you are offering help to a tightly defined group such as women victims of violence, black women or gay men.
- Congruent; (see below).

By 'congruent' I don't mean that the advertising has to be simply honest in its portrayal of the service you are offering - although this is absolutely essential if you are to establish and maintain credibility. It has to be 'in the manner of' your agency in the way it portrays your mission, aims and objectives. This is because the advertising you produce may be the first point of contact a person has with your service and your potential clients are already forming opinions about what kind of people you are and what it might be like to ask you for help as a result of this publicity material. In short this material is the first part of the process whereby you **structure** your helping relationship with your clients.

A brief word about structuring
Structuring is the process whereby the client and counsellor draw up the 'rules' of the relationship. This happens in an unspoken way in all 'relationship episodes', however brief.

When you walk down the street and see an acquaintance approach, both of you quickly negotiate by means of a series of rapid glances and bodily movements. By the time you meet, you will have decided how long you are prepared to have a meeting for, roughly what the meeting will be about and how intimate you will be with each other. Will you warmly greet each other and embrace or say a quick 'Hello' and pass by? If one of you gets it wrong, there will be an embarrassing and awkward moment. We align our expectations of each relationship episode every time we meet someone and we know all too painfully what happens when one of us gets it wrong.

We will see in Chapter 6 how to structure your relationship with the client when they start a counselling relationship, i.e. when the first telephone interview starts with a given caller. However, the process of structuring your relationship with the client started long before that. It started the moment there was any contact between the agency and the client. It was at that moment that the client started to build expectations about any future relationship s/he might have with you:
- Is the agency organised and reliable or slapdash?
- Will the counsellors be warm and friendly, or cold and authoritarian?
- Are the helpers 'expert advisers' or 'equal partners' in the helping process?
- Do the counsellors listen to the clients or tell the clients what to do?
- Will clients behaviour be judged?
- Is the service confidential - can it be trusted?

Does your publicity lead your potential clients to have an accurate idea of what your agency is like. Is it **congruent**?

The process of structuring continues if the reader of your publicity decides to call your agency or pay a visit to your premises. What do they find on first contact? What does the voice on the phone or the entrance to your building tell them? Again, the questions are:
- *Is* the agency organised and reliable or slapdash?
- *Will* the counsellors be warm and friendly or cold and authoritarian?
- *Are* the helpers 'expert advisers' or 'equal partners' in the helping process?
- *Do* the counsellors listen to the clients or tell the clients what to do?
- *Will* clients behaviour be judged?
- *Is* the service confidential - can it be trusted?

And so it goes on at every point of contact - reception areas, reception staff, manner of greeting; you name it. Everything that happens to a potential client is helping them decide what you're like and whether they want to be helped by you. The publicity material you use should not try to 'sell' your agency, but help clients align their expectations so that they will not be disappointed or disoriented when they finally arrive in the counselling session - whether on the phone or face to face. Your publicity should be congruent.

Given the need for congruence in publicity, here is a checklist to help you assess the image you are getting across:
Agency name:
- Are you happy that the agency name gives the right impression?
- Does your logo give an accurate impression of the values and mission of the agency?

Publicity:
- Is it clear about the kind, range and availability of services you offer?
- Does it give a realistic picture and not raise false expectations - e.g. have you the staff and resources to deliver what you claim?

Distribution:

- Do you place publicity where it will reach as wide a range of potential clients as possible?
- Have you identified potential client groups, what they read and where they meet?
- Do you use a wide range of media?
- Do you exploit free publicity, e.g. local press 'advertorials', press releases, etc?
- Do you give talks to interested organisations and those which represent your potential client groups?

Personal safety

All organisations must have a concern for the safety of their staff. This will be particularly true of organisations which require people to work in the evenings or at night. You must decide when and where you feel most vulnerable and ask your agency for protection.

If you're not sure what this might mean, here are some ideas:

Counsellor anonymity - in addition to protecting the identity of your callers, you may well expect your privacy to be respected too. Is there an agency policy which says that your personal details must not be given to anyone without your permission, and never to a client even with your permission?

Getting home - if you are expected to work shifts that begin or end at night, are you given a lift or escorted home or to a place of safety?

At the office - does agency policy say that no-one must be in the office alone? Are there panic buttons located in all rooms where you might meet clients or strangers on your own? Do you feel secure when you are on duty?

In Training: Personal safety of agency counsellors, whether volunteers or not, should be a high priority. If the agency is unclear about the issues, then let your workers have an input. This exercise might be a useful starting place. In any event it will help individuals take some responsibility for their own safety too.

Method:
• Suggest a mini counselling session (15 minutes each way) on personal safety. Split group into pairs to explore their feelings on the issue. Share in the large group and be aware that some people may have had distressing personal experiences.
• Brainstorm ways in which a) the agency may make a safe working environment in terms of premises and policy, and b) individuals may behave in safe ways.
Learning Points:
• How do the suggestions made compare with current policy?
• Do make sure that management is permanently responsive to the legitimate safety concerns of workers.

The issue of personal safety is not simply about ensuring your physical safety, but also about ensuring that you *feel* safe whilst working. You can hardly be expected to create a safe secure space for your clients if you do not feel safe and secure yourself. Your feelings of insecurity will be detected by clients and may well rub off on them. Evenso make sure that your need for a safe working environment doesn't turn your agency premises into a prison - you need to feel comfortable too!

Equality of access and opportunity
It should go without saying in 1996 that every public service agency should have an equal opportunities policy or statement. In telephone counselling it is particularly important to consider your position regarding equality of opportunity and access because some agencies whilst offering a 'publicly' available service, might wish to restrict access for any one of a number of reasons:
• They wish to restrict access to a particular 'thematic' group, i.e. amputees and their families or those suffering from MS.
• They wish to restrict access to a particular self-identifying group, i.e. gay men or black people.
• They wish to restrict access for safety reasons, i.e. women's aid.
• They wish to restrict access in order to free valuable lines for 'bona fide' callers.

Other telephone counselling services may wish to restrict access for a different set of reasons:
- Funding, e.g. a local authority run service may not be able to help a caller from outside a given geographical area.
- Commercial reasons, e.g. an EAP will only take calls from those who subscribe to its services.

Within the restrictions imposed in the ways illustrated above, the various services will wish to operate an access policy for callers and workers that is free from discrimination in terms of race, religion, disability, class, age, sexual orientation, gender, etc., wherever appropriate. Along with the complications caused by such access considerations, it has been found that black people, disabled people and males particularly from working class backgrounds are under-represented in counselling. Your agency should ensure that there is at least equal access to:
- Recruitment procedures and training - for potential staff.
- Agency services - for clients.
- Premises - both clients and staff.
- Publicity - is it distributed in places used by black people, or accessible to disabled people, for example?

This easier said than done, since many a fair equal opportunities policy fails to be implemented. The first task is to raise awareness regarding issues of equality. The second is to be active in pursuing these issues. This can be achieved by:
- Thoughtful development of agency policy to actively embrace non-discriminatory aims and promote non-discriminatory practice.
- Careful preparation and monitoring of publicity and recruitment procedures.
- Deliberate focusing on issues of oppression and equal opportunities in training.
- Careful attention to developing non-discriminatory office procedures.
- Continual monitoring and evaluation of the effectiveness of these interventions.

In Training: It is important to ensure that equal opportunities issues are given a high profile.

Method:

• Split the group into threes and get them to share experiences of oppression, discrimination, inequality.

• Ask the group what they think the needs of oppressed groups might be as far as your service is concerned. Collate views on flipchart, discuss and compare to agency policy.

• Pay careful attention to racist or sexist attitudes and language used by trainees.

Learning Points:

• Be prepared to learn from trainees, especially if they identify themselves as members of an oppressed group.

• It is good practice to have mixture of people in your organisation as an active demonstration that your policy is working.

Some agencies will have policies and practices designed to make themselves particularly user-friendly to some oppressed groups by having, e.g. special access via minicom, a large number of black counsellors, mainly women counsellors, etc. Other agencies will prefer to make access easier still for certain oppressed groups by designating themselves a specialist service, e.g. women only, gay advice line, etc. Make sure your agency publicity carries an equal opportunities or anti-oppression statement. Don't work for the agency if you don't agree with its position on equal opportunities.

Equality of opportunity and access is, as I mentioned above, easier said than done, since the best made policies will encounter situations in practice which present individuals and agencies with particular dilemmas. These dilemmas often take the form of having to enforce a restricted access system whist staying true to the values of counselling. Turning people away from a telephone agency is, in some senses, much more difficult than turning them away from an agency offering face-to-face help. Turning male victims/survivors of abuse away from a helpline established by women to help women survivors, or turning male victims of rape away from a rape crisis line are good examples of this dilemma. Another dilemma that counsellors feel burdened by is their desire to help, set against the limits of funding. These and other similar dilemmas are best dealt with in training by presenting trainees with role plays or discussions focused on these issues. Agency policy should be as unequivocal as possible, offering clear guidelines which workers have developed, supporting telephone counsellors, not giving them another burden.

It is vital that those we turn away are treated respectfully and wherever possible actively referred on to another helping agency, one where their needs can be met without equivocation. Referral skills are an essential part of your helping repertoire, see p.35.

Insurance
It is increasingly important that agencies and their workers enjoy proper protection through appropriate insurance cover. This is easy to arrange through an insurance broker for public liability (a visitor may trip over a loose piece of carpet) and BAC will give advice on professional liability (if a client claims s/he was damaged by your advice, guidance or counselling).

Abusive calls and silent calls
The skills required to deal with these types of call are dealt with in Chapter 7. Here we are attending to the issue of whether your agency has a policy which clearly explains your responsibilities to the caller and the agencies responsibilities to you. For example:
  • Who can end a call?
  • Are you allowed to put the phone down, or must you always wait for the client to do so?
  • How long must you wait in silence before deciding to put the phone down on a caller?
  • Must you listen to an abusive or threatening caller?
  • Does your agency have anything to say about 'hoax' calls, (see p.134) i.e:
    What are they?
    Who defines them?
    How can you recognise one?

What do you do when you think you've got one?
• Who is your first line of support should you receive a difficult call?

In Training: Make the issue of abusive or threatening calls the subject of a mini counselling session.
Method:
• Split the group into pairs and ask them to help each other explore their feelings about abusive, threatening and silent calls. Share in large group.
Learning Point:
• This exercise can open up difficult and painful experiences and feelings for people. Be prepared for distressing experiences to be shared. Allow plenty of time for debriefing or 'coming down' after this session.

Every agency policy should create a secure space in which you can offer a helping relationship to the callers. It is the agency's way of providing the core conditions necessary for the provision of a good telephone counselling relationship. If you are unsure how to act in any set of circumstances, your first stop is your agency policy. If that doesn't help you should *act in the way which feels right for you* and seek support as soon as the call or situation is over. The same goes for the next section.

Referrals
To feel completely supported by an agency policy it should tell us what the limits of the agency service are. This includes helping us decide who we should accept referrals from and to whom we may refer clients and under what circumstances. Along with agency guidelines on referral we should also have a keen sense of our own limits of competence and our personal emotional limits. How and to whom do we refer when we think we can't help or can't cope.

To help with basic referral strategy, the agency should provide a list of approved referral routes into and out of the agency. You should also feel that you have the skills (developed in training) to receive a referral with confidence and refer a client on without leaving the client feeling they have been seen as 'difficult', rejected or unworthy.

There may be many reasons why we would refer a caller on to another helper or another agency, or even wish to turn a particular caller away (see pp 35 & 69). In all cases we should refer the caller so that they do not feel devalued or put down by the experience. The whole referral experience is one where the caller should feel that their experience has been added to and enhanced, not diminished; one where they feel cared for not passed from pillar to post like an unwanted bundle. The caller should feel as though they can call you or your agency next week with a different problem and be accepted anew.

In his book *An Incomplete Guide to Referral issues for Counsellors* (see p. 35) Steve Williams looks at a wide range of referral situations and offers many suggestions for training.

Today's duty - are you ready?
I started off this chapter by comparing preparing for telephone counselling with preparing to go on a long car journey. So far we've done the equivalent of checking that the car is road worthy and that we are properly qualified and insured to drive.

What about personal 'here-and-now' checking?
- Have you been drinking alcohol?
- Have you had a sensible meal?
- Do you feel tired?
- Do you want to go to the toilet?
- Are you dressed comfortably?
- Have you 'checked in' with yourself, preparing yourself for the next few hours on the telephone, clearing your mind of all of your personal issues and telephone baggage?

We would do all of these things automatically before driving a long distance, and generally speaking I wouldn't start a counselling duty if I didn't think I was fit to drive. The same kind of checks apply, because I need to feel physically and emotionally capable of doing the job. Both driving and counselling are very responsible activities. Lives can be at stake, so I try to make sure I'm in a fit state to do the job.

In particular, counsellors need to be sure that they are emotionally capable of providing a supportive relationship on any given day. Sometimes it isn't possible, since fate has a habit of throwing up unexpected events in everyone's life - counsellors included. Family illness, bereavement, unemployment, any sort of bad news can cast doubt on your capacity to help others. And it needn't be just bad news which can throw you off track - I pity the poor client who is counselled by me just after I've been left a million in a will! The point is, only I can really tell how I feel, and I must responsibly ask myself before each duty whether I can be a good enough counsellor.

Most days are neither desperately bad nor fantastically good. They are firmly stuck in that grey area in between - could be better, could be worse. Usually my task is to make sure that I can leave issues in my personal life behind. I don't want to visit them on my clients. They're coming to me for help.

It is good to feel supported by agency policy, fellow counsellors and agency management. To know that if I say, 'No, I can't do it today', they will understand that I have my own and the client's best interests at the centre of my actions.

Briefing
Some agencies have a briefing meeting before a duty shift begins, or when one shift 'hands over' to another. These meetings are good vehicles to give information regarding 'local' conditions that day, e.g. if anyone is sick or absent, if regular callers have been on the line, if any special situations or orders prevail, such as listening out for a particular caller, etc.

Such meetings also help to reinforce agency policy, introduce new workers, or identify shift/day leaders or supervisors. You may feel that they only make real sense in large helpline organisations, but I believe that briefings are good practice whatever the size of the agency. It gives telephone counsellors an opportunity to 'check in', do some of the self-preparation mentioned above, and generally get ready for action. We often forget that telephone work is essentially an isolated and isolating activity. This can be ameliorated to some extent by attending to our needs for social contact and company at least for ten to fifteen minutes before we go on the lines.

If your agency doesn't have briefing meetings, check out the possibility if you feel it would help telephone counsellors to improve the service you give your clients. You may also be interested to read about debriefing meetings in Chapter 8.

6 On the Telephone

In Chapter 2, I explained why it is so important to define the activity and why I decided to use the title 'Using Counselling Skills on the Telephone'. What follows in this chapter is my best effort to describe the interaction between counselling skills and the telephone. As I wrote, again in Chapter 2, there is no reason why 'Telephone Counselling' in the genuinely therapeutic sense of the word can't be offered by a properly qualified and supervised person, however the skills I will refer to in this chapter are not in themselves sufficient to offer 'Telephone Counselling'.

In Chapter 5, I ran through the reasons why good training is important and what training would be appropriate for those who wish to offer counselling skills. Reading this chapter and trying out the ideas in isolation, in the absence of a trainer, is similarly insufficient preparation for offering either counselling or counselling skills on the telephone. Chapter 11 gives a more detailed account of training at Family Contact Line and may help you put some of these ideas into a training context, or build and enhance your own agency's training experience.

The idea is that this chapter, indeed the whole book, should supplement your experience as a counsellor, as a user of counselling skills on the phone or in your training and preparation for that work.

'Core' counselling conditions
In 1957 Carl Rogers wrote a paper in which he argued that certain conditions need to be in place in a relationship before any helping activity can be effective. He wrote that there are six conditions for therapeutic or helpful change and that these conditions must exist and continue over a period of time. Three of these conditions are now referred to as the 'core' conditions, but I will include all six here because although it might be assumed by face-to-face workers that some of these conditions are 'automatic', we cannot afford the same luxury when working on the telephone.

The six conditions that are necessary and sufficient for therapeutic change (Rogers 1957):

1 Two persons are in psychological contact.

2 The first, the client, is in a vulnerable or anxious state.

3 The second person, the therapist (counsellor) is congruent or integrated (genuine) in the relationship.

4 The counsellor experiences unconditional positive regard (acceptance) for the client.

5 The counsellor experiences empathic understanding of the client's world and viewpoint, and tries to communicate this to the client.

6 The counsellor is able to communicate these conditions to the client to a minimal degree.

Much has been written about the three conditions (3,4 and 5) that people consider to be most obviously important (the three core conditions) and a good understanding of them is an essential basis for sound effective counselling practice (whether on the telephone or face-to-face). However, I suggest that it is important for counsellors and users of counselling skills on the telephone to look at all six of these conditions to see how they might impact upon telephone work.

Psychological contact - What it is and how to maintain it on the telephone.
We might take it for granted when sitting in the same room as our client, looking at them, making occasional eye contact with them, that we are in psychological contact with them. Carl Rogers meant much more than simply being in the same room with another person when he wrote about psychological contact. We all know the difference between simply being in someone's presence and actually being in relationship with them.

Although psychological contact is wider than just visual contact, most of us do rely rather heavily on making visual contact in order to feel that we are 'there' with someone. Take away that visual contact and suddenly we're not so sure. On the telephone we have

to make psychological contact and maintain it without the benefit of vision. In crude terms this means that we have to use our ears and our voice more in order to answer some fundamental questions:
- How do I know if there is anyone there?
- How do I find out if the caller is a client?
- How do I establish 'quality contact' with her/him?

If there is a pause in the conversation:
- How do I know the client is still there?
- How do I know the client still wants to talk?
- How do I know how comfortable the client feels?
- How does the client know I'm still here?
- How does the client know I'm still listening and interested?

Once I have established that the client is still there and that s/he knows that I am too, and since I can't see the client,
- How long can I leave it before I need to check again?

In Training: Introduce the notion of psychological contact and how it may be differently established on the phone.
Method:
- Split group into twos and threes and get them to answer the above questions. Share answers in large group and discuss.
Learning Points:
- Those trainees who are already trained as face-to-face counsellors could be asked to share their experience of making and maintaining contact face-to-face.

These points are developed further later in this chapter and at various stages throughout the book.

Sound gestures
Psychologists have various terms for the ways we communicate in parallel to language. I suggest that this area of human communications could be referred to as 'sound gestures'. That is to say looking at the

way we use sounds to communicate beyond words in speech. When we can see the other person we use gestures that can be seen, from crude arm waving to the fabled twinkle in the eye. When we can't see the person we're talking to we still communicate 'beyond the words', but by using our voice, breathing, making non-vocal sounds (tut-tutting or smacking our lips etc.), speeding up, slowing down, speaking loudly and softly and being silent.

Clients and helper/listener/counsellors

Rogers' next two conditions concern themselves with the structure of the relationship between two people, i.e. what sort of relationship is it?
- Is it a helping relationship?
- If so, what sort of helping relationship?
- Is it mutually negotiated?
- Is one person structurally more powerful than the other?
- Is one person an expert?
- Is one person desperate?
- Is one person a helper/listener/counsellor?
- Is one person being helped/listened to/a client?

It is important that everyone concerned with helping, both helpers and those being helped know what sort of helping relationship they are in. Their expectations of what is possible and appropriate are more likely to be met, clients stand less chance of being disappointed or abused, and helpers are more likely to feel effective and valued. On the telephone, we must work just that little bit harder to ensure that it really is a client we are talking to, not someone wanting another type of telephone service. The only way to make sure that we don't miss any possible clients is to treat all callers as clients.

This policy of 'all callers are clients' has many ramifications, for example, we must employ all of our expertise in sensing and understanding verbal communication and 'sound gestures'. When assessing client needs we must be careful that we don't jump to premature conclusions. We also must be clear about our position on 'hoax calls' (see page 134). As soon as the status of the caller is known, we should take all reasonable care to explain to them the nature of the helping that is on offer, including the cost (if any) and the limits (time, confidentiality, who can end the session, etc.). These issues are looked at in Chapter 5 pp 66-68).

The British Association for Counselling also points out that the people that we are trying to help have a right to know what sort of relationship they are getting into. If we are using counselling skills, we should let our clients know and in the Code of Ethics and Practice for Counsellors the BAC make it clear that it is unethical to practice when the client does not fully understand that they are a client in counselling. So it would not be ethical to proceed with a caller who says 'I want some advice please, but don't try any of that counselling on me will you? I've had that before and I didn't like it at all!'

In Training: It is essential that trainees understand the nature of the helping relationship they are being trained to deliver, and how to let callers know this.

Method:
• Start off with some of the questions on the facing page, getting trainees to debate them in groups.
• Ask trainees to write out on flipcharts a concise definition of the agency's services. Display and discuss in large group.
• Ask trainees to develop some scripted statements to get the message across in as natural a way as possible. Do this in twos and threes. Display and discuss.

Learning Points:
It is important that trainees feel that they have an active role in developing these statements. Make sure that alternatives are allowed and that individual differences are heard and valued, e.g. someone who says, 'I couldn't say that - I'd feel daft, it just isn't me.'

Empathy
Empathy is the effort of trying to see the world of another person through their own eyes. It has been described as walking in someone else's shoes, understanding how someone else feels and thinks,

sensitively entering into another person's private world of special meanings and so on.

Some books refer to 'accurate empathy' or 'empathic understanding'. I'm not sure that these words actually add to my understanding of empathy since I'm sure that *inaccurate* empathy would be of use to no-one, nor indeed would empathic *non-understanding*. What we can say about empathy, however, is that it involves appreciating and understanding both the thoughts and the feelings of the client, both the content and the process, the 'words' and the 'music'.

Being empathic is what many refer to as 'active listening' and in face-to-face counselling that involves looking at the client as well as listening to them. In fact picking up clues any way you can as to what the client is thinking and how they are feeling. On the telephone you will be working with a restricted set of information, so you must learn to 'tune in' to the client by putting all of the sound-only clues to much better use than in the average face-to-face session.

Acceptance

Many clients come for counselling because they are afraid of being judged by others (maybe parents or friends) for something they have done or are planning to do. Callers may well be drawn to telephone counselling because it affords them yet another protection from judgement, i.e. they cannot be seen or identified. It is crucial that telephone counsellors provide an atmosphere of total acceptance in which clients can feel free to explore their troubles without fear of being judged. American books often refer to this core condition as *unconditional positive regard.* Although this is a bit of a mouthful, its meaning can be made clear. The essence of it is that counsellors must see their clients as worthy (positive regard) regardless of what that person may have done (unconditional). Seeing someone as worthy does not mean that you have to approve of their behaviour or admire them. Simply see them as a human being of equal value.

Some British books call it *non-judgemental warmth*, another good term since it puts the rather neutral 'non-judgemental' bit next to the more positive 'warmth'. This also helps us break down the idea into two component skills - firstly the absence of judgement, secondly the communication of warmth. This core condition is not just the absence or suspension of judgement, but also the positive feeling of warmth towards the other person as a valuable worthy person. Many clients come for counselling in the first place because their feeling of worth has been damaged by painful experiences. By offering this core condition we can help heal those hurts.

Genuineness

Genuineness is the last of the three 'core' conditions written about by Carl Rogers. It involves the helper acting in a way that is honest, true to themselves, without front, mask or facade, without adopting a role such as 'expert' or 'teacher' and so on. Rogers described it as being 'transparently real' and includes being one's self in ways which may not be seen as ideal for counselling, for example, having 'negative' thoughts and feelings.

Within the core condition of genuineness lies a fundamental challenge to us all to be ourselves; fallible, vulnerable and even gullible, (see Chapter 7) complete with all manner of feelings. We must be our real self with our clients in a way which does not harm, diminish or take away from their own self worth. In this way they may come to see that it is safe to be themselves here in this session. As telephone counsellors we must not give up on being genuine simply because our clients can't see us. We have to invest our whole telephone presence with our voice gestures that communicate genuineness. *Rogers also said that these conditions were both necessary and sufficient.*

Necessary: This means that therapeutic change will only take place if all three core conditions are present - if one is missing, change may take place but it will not be therapeutic. Of course there are many types of change - some positive and sought after, some negative and unhelpful. These 'core conditions' may be present in these situations to a lesser degree, but only when all three are there will the change be therapeutic.

Sufficient : If all three are present, even by accident, therapeutic change may take place even if it was not planned for. How many times have we found it really easy to talk over our problems and feel really helped in the most unlikely places? Also some people seem to be 'natural' listeners and find that others will seek them out to talk to. These are occasions when the core conditions are provided in an accidental, informal or unplanned way.

The core conditions are qualities rather than skills and other counsellors have tried to break down the core conditions and the therapeutic process in general into skills. The idea is to break down these qualities of helping into small enough parts to be able to understand them so that we can improve through repeated practice. This helps take the mystery out of providing a good quality helping relationship. The important ingredient needed to turn repeated practice into effective training is good quality, responsible**feedback**.

Skills

Since Carl Rogers wrote about these therapeutic conditions, there has been a lively debate concerning the necessity and sufficiency of them. Some practitioners believe that they are necessary and sufficient, whilst some believe they are necessary but may not be sufficient. Although many counsellors are trained in face-to-face settings to use the Rogerian core conditions, many writers and trainers prefer to use Gerard Egan's (The Skilled Helper 1975 & 1982) three stage model to identify the skills required for telephone counselling. Rogers' ideas on the core conditions were developed by Egan, who incorporated the three core conditions into a model in which Rogers' core conditions form the first of three stages.

If you do hold with the view that the core conditions are all that's needed for therapeutic change, you may still find the next section useful since, although I have used Egan's Stage 1 skills as a framework to look at telephone work, I don't veer too far from Rogers' ideas. Indeed some may think that there is no need to use Egan's model as a framework. Either way, my intention is to be *inclusive* not exclusive in the next section.

Egan's three stage helping model.
• Stage 1
Exploration: Creating a warm trusting relationship with the client, enabling the client to explore whatever they choose. Entering the client's 'frame of reference' (looking at the world from the client's point of view).
Skills: Active listening, communicating empathy, genuineness and non-judgemental warmth, acknowledging and reflecting feelings, paraphrasing, focusing and clarifying.

• Stage 2
Understanding: Helping the client see their situation with new understanding, from different perspectives, with alternative information.
Skills: All of Stage 1 skills plus summarising, linking and integrating issues into themes, offering new perspectives, sharing, challenging, immediacy (looking at what's happening right here and now between you and the client) and goal setting.

• Stage 3
Action: Looking with the client at possible ways of acting in this situation. Assessing risks and possible outcomes. Helping the client evaluate the effectiveness of their new behaviour.
Skills: All of the skills of stages 1 & 2 plus brainstorming, creative thinking, planning, implementing and evaluating plans.

Many of these skills can be learned in a face-to-face context and transferred just as easily to a telephone context. So as far as some skills are concerned there need be no special training for using counselling skills on the telephone, but as I mentioned in Chapter 1, there are *some* special considerations to be made for telephone work. For those readers who have had little or no training, I will expand on each of these skills using telephone examples as I go. Wherever possible I will also give training suggestions.

There are two elements to all counselling skills - discrimination and communication. **Discrimination** is the picking up of the relevant information (from your client, yourself or any other source) and **communication** is the skill of letting your client know what information you've picked up. For example if the skill in question is active listening, there are two components - discrimination and communication:

• Discrimination is the listening part - not just to the words, but picking up all of the subtle nuances between the words, listening to the tone of voice, breathing patterns, trembling voice, etc, trying to sense the feelings behind the story.

• Communication on the other hand, is the feeding back to your client that you have heard and understood what s/he is saying and feeling, checking that you are correct and indicating that it's the client's turn to talk.

The problems relating to maintaining psychological contact only arise when working on the phone. The establishment and maintenance of this contact requires high quality listening and a fair amount of talking from the counsellor.

Making contact

In order to make contact and establish that you have a bona-fide client, most people have a comfortable telephone answering routine worked out. *'Hello, Pete Sanders' Telephone Counselling Service here, can I help you?'* or something similar will do. Don't worry if your opening lines begin to sound over-used, thousands of volunteers have been saying *'Hello, Samaritans, can I help?'* for well over 30 years without putting callers off.

Maintaining contact

Once you have established that you have a bona-fide client rather than a wrong number, your next task is to keep in psychological contact with your client. In face-to-face situations, this is made easier because you can use a number of sight-dependent actions such as:

• Looking at your client
• Making eye contact
• Smiling
• Nodding your head
• Making gestures with your hands
• Leaning forward in your chair

On the phone we are restricted to maintaining this contact with verbal or sound-dependent methods only. When we can't see the person we are talking to, we become very sensitive to the way time passes in a conversation. Seconds seem like minutes and minutes seem to stretch on forever.

In Training: Making and maintaining contact on the phone is the first new skill most trainees will have to grapple with.
Method:
• Split up into pairs and get one in each pair to close their eyes and to guess when a minute of silence has elapsed. Or ask each pair start a conversation with their eyes closed and prime one person to lapse into silence after a minute or so.
• The second person then guesses when one minute has elapsed. Feedback and discuss.
• *Learning Points:*
Silences are difficult enough to deal with face-to-face, so expect this exercise to generate lots of feelings, from, 'How ridiculous!' to, 'Great, how challenging!'

This effect is not limited to counsellors. Clients feel it too; so we must work hard to keep contact with our clients so that they have a safe, secure atmosphere in which to receive the rest of our counselling skills. The only way to do this is to maintain our presence verbally by talking more and making more sounds in general than we would face-to-face. Typical ways to do this are by saying:

• Uh-huh	• Mmm
• Yes	• Please go on
• I see	• Right
• Ah-hah	
• Do you want to say more about that?	

These responses can be varied or combined ad infinitum eg: 'Yes, please go on,' or 'Ah-hah, I see, right,' etc.

Stage 1 Skills: Active listening and communicating empathy
Active listening is one of the key ingredients of empathy. It is not possible to be empathic if you are not actively listening. In face-to-face situations, active listening requires that you attend with your whole being to everything that the client is trying to communicate to you. That means using all of your senses, including sight. We get lots of information about the client and his/her feelings from the way they look and present themselves, their posture, their facial expressions, their gestures etc.

On the telephone we miss all of that and at the same time we get many vocal and breathing noises amplified above normal. This can be distracting. So on the phone we need to work a little bit harder to overcome the disadvantages of this restricted set of information. How can this be overcome? We must tune in to everything available to sense what the client is thinking and feeling. For example:

- Voice 'quality' - tone, pitch and volume.
  Is it a strong or weak voice? Old or young? Confident or timid?
- Breathing noises - sobbing, chattering teeth, sighing, holding their breath or crying.
  Is the client sad, hurt, afraid or angry?
- Speed of talking.
  Is the client rushing and nervous or slow and relaxed? Speeding and excited or sluggish and depressed?
- Other vocalisations such as laughter, snorting or grunting.
  Is the client happy, sad, furious? Do they sound genuine?
- Background noises.
  Is the client alone or do they keep getting interrupted? How does this affect them?
- Silence.
  What is happening? Is the client pausing for thought?

The other key ingredient in empathy is communication. It's no good me sitting on the end of the phone being the most empathic person in the world if I'm not communicating this to the client. The core conditions must be *experienced* by the client.

Reflection

The basic method of empathy is to reflect the content of the client's utterances back to them. By content I mean both the storyline content and the feelings content - this isn't necessarily spoken. (This is where all the jokes about counsellors nodding and saying "Uh huh, so you feel angry," after the client has just thrown the chair out of the window come from.)

In Training: It can help to start off by looking at feelings.
Method:
There are several ways to focus on feelings;
•Start by developing a vocabulary of feelings. Split into twos, brainstorming as many feeling words as possible. Share and collate in large group. If someone doesn't understand a particular word, get the person who brainstormed it to explain.
•Use role plays to help trainees identify feelings which they have problems hearing or experiencing. (People that can't bear someone else to be angry often have difficulty in managing their own anger.)
Learning Points:
• Trainees can get hooked on getting the accuracy of the content of the client's story right at the expense of paying attention to the client's feelings. Putting the spotlight onto feelings early on can help stop this.

The ability to give good reflections without sounding like a parrot is simply a matter of making the activity natural to you. Don't judge the art of reflection by your own wooden first attempts. That's a bit like saying that ballroom dancing is just a matter of putting one foot after another, trying it yourself for five minutes and then saying that it looks stupid.

The real dancing starts when you can blend together technique and natural self. Not only does it look as though the dancers are floating effortlessly on air, it actually feels like that too! The same goes for all counselling skills - reflecting in particular. When you get the hang of it, it becomes an effortless second nature; not wooden at all. How do you achieve this? The two ingredients of technique and natural self must be brought together by a process of *practice* and *feedback*.

In Training: If possible use a cassette tape recorder to help with the development of skills. Although trainees can be anxious about being recorded, it is worthwhile persevering since much more can be achieved in a short space of time.
Method:
• In pairs, start off by recording short snippets - say two minutes - of the start of a counselling interview. Ask the counsellors to concentrate on accurate reflection of the client's statements.
• Then play back and listen carefully to the client's statements and the counsellor's responses. Is the counsellor's reflection accurate and complete?
• Move on to longer segments. Concentrate on getting the group to recognise complete and accurate reflection and giving good feedback to each other.
Learning Points:
• Using a tape recorder can be developed into a number of spin-off exercises.
• Ask the group to give feedback on the individual qualities each counsellor brings to the art of reflection. As each counsellor gains confidence in their ability to be accurate on both a feelings and storyline level, emphasise the individual, natural qualities in the feedback.

Being empathic is quite difficult to start off with, and you may encounter some common problems. For example, many clients start off their first contact with a counsellor in a great rush with a torrent of words. They are understandably anxious and try to tell you their whole story in one block at the front end of the session. Your task is to be empathic, seeing the client's world from their point of view. Since the key skill is to communicate this understanding to the client and the basic method is reflection, the problem is how to listen actively, remember, accurately reflect and check for accuracy, when the client won't stop talking to let you get a word in edgeways.

Many people believe that listening passively without doing anything other than saying 'Yes', 'I see', or 'Uh huh', and nodding your head is enough. I do not believe it is. In the first place, we have to maintain contact with the client verbally on the phone and if they are talking all the time we can't do this. In the second place the key skill is *active* listening, not passive listening. This means encouraging the client to say more and reflecting the content of their statements so as to give the message:

> *'I'm listening to what you're saying and trying to understand. I will demonstrate this to you by letting you know that I heard what you just said. Here it is - have I got it right?'*

The only way I have found to do this is to interrupt the client. Even when they are in full flow. This technique, once mastered, will enable you to break up the client's story into manageable chunks so that you can do a reasonable job of reflecting and communicating empathy.

You may worry that you client will be put off. You may worry that your client may lose the thread of their story. You may worry that your client will think you rude and disrespectful. It is my contention that you should interrupt in order to communicate the message:

> *'What you are saying is so important that I must slow you down to make sure I catch it all.'*

This is a respectful thing to say. You can also try saying:

> *'I realise that you want to tell me your story, but I can't keep up with you. Could you slow down a little and let me check every now and then to make sure I've got it right.'*

As well as enabling you to maintain contact, these interruptions will help you establish a pattern of *client statement - counsellor response*. This pattern will make any work on the telephone easier since the eye contact we normally use in order to manage a conversation is not available to us on the phone. When a comfortable *talk - listen - response* pattern is set up early in the interview, the client and counsellor can settle down to build up their relationship. Setting up this pattern is another example of **structuring** (see Chapter 5).

Structuring

Structuring is a way of aligning the client's expectations with what you are providing and when used to set up a pattern in this way, structuring will in itself communicate certain messages about the counselling relationship to the client:

- •I (the counsellor) will listen and you (the client) will talk.
- •You and your world are the centre of both this session and my complete attention.
- •I am trying so hard to understand what you are thinking and feeling that I constantly check to make sure that I've got it right.
- •I am not setting myself up as an expert.
- •You are the expert on the subject of you.
- •I am paying attention to both your story and your feelings.

If the client continues to talk too fast or for too long for you to grasp and reflect the key points, interrupt again. Try

> *'I know I keep interrupting, but it's so important that I understand as much as possible.'*

or

> *'I realise you want to get this off your chest. That is why I'm interrupting you to make sure I've got it right.'*

If the client's flow is stopped, you will be aware of it, although in my experience this rarely happens - if a client really is bursting they can easily overcome a few interruptions. If the client is irritated or distracted by your interruptions, you will notice (sometimes they will tell you!). Again, this rarely happens in my experience, but if it does try saying:

> *'I can see that my interruptions are irritating you. If you could leave some gaps when you're talking, I can check to see if I'm understanding you correctly.'*

The 'technique' part of structuring is to:
- reflect what you see and hear,
- be open and genuine,
- not let the client get too far ahead of you by talking for too long otherwise you'll lose the thread.

The 'natural' part of structuring is achieved by practising until it becomes second nature. When I first sat in front of the wheel of a car and tried to drive off, I found it so difficult that I couldn't even begin to imagine how I could take my hands off the wheel to change gear, let alone look in the rear view mirror. After much practice I can now drive and turn on, and listen to, the radio or talk to the person sitting next to me, without even thinking about it. I am a confident, relaxed and natural driver and my driving style reflects my personality.

When learning a new skill we start off from a position of *unconscious incompetence* - we don't know which skills are needed nor do we know which skills we have or don't have. We move on to *conscious incompetence* when we start recognising the skills that we need but don't have. Next comes *conscious competence* where we have to concentrate like crazy in order to keep the skill going and doing it feels really awkward and artificial. Finally we arrive at *unconscious competence*, the 'radio-on-driving' I mentioned above. This is when an activity which once felt awkward, wooden and artificial, becomes second nature.

Paraphrasing, focusing and clarifying
These three skills are complementary to basic reflection and together with reflection form your 'empathy repertoire'. When used together they turn reflection from mere parroting of the client's words into a powerful method of communicating your real effort to understand the client. This understanding can help the client move forward since you will be helping them clarify their often blurred and tangled issues.

Paraphrasing is the skill of summarising what the client is saying. This summarising can be of what the client has just said in their last utterance, what the client has been saying during the session, or even over several sessions. Paraphrasing the client's statements over a longer period may often reveal patterns in the client's issues which they may find helpful.

When paraphrasing it is sometimes best to use your own words and sometimes best to use the client's own words. Using the client's own words can sometimes capture a power that becomes diluted if you use your own. You must develop a sense of good judgement to know how best to paraphrase in any given situation.

Focusing is sensing the key issues in what the client is saying from the way the client is talking. Clients do sometimes say *'This is the most important thing'*, but they may not be sure, or often they don't mean it and sometimes even when they do, their tone of voice gives a signal that something else is important too. Helping a client focus on the important issues is sometimes difficult on the phone because people have a tendency to ramble on over the phone, so you may have to develop your ability to interrupt to help your focusing. When you start out in counselling it's often good to be cautious or tentative when helping a client focus on the most important issues. Focusing is a skill which takes a fair degree of practice to get right, since if you get it wrong you may end up *telling* the client what's most important rather than *checking* with them that your hunch might be even vaguely right.

Clarifying is not quite as self-explanatory as it sounds. There are at least two possible definitions of this skill.
• Firstly it can be the activity of helping your client to unravel a tangle, see clearly through a foggy patch, hear an 'inner whisper' more distinctly. This involves accurate active listening and clear thinking on your part. It is not a case of being smarter than the caller, simply that since it is *not your problem*, you may be able to get a slightly different angle on it.
• Secondly, it can be when you are trying to clarify what the caller has said *for yourself* because you don't understand. Sometimes a caller is so distressed that they do not make sense, however hard you listen. In such circumstances it is important that you make every effort to understand them by trying to clarify exactly what they are

saying. Client-callers often find this very helpful since they may be muddled themselves and you asking for clarification for yourself helps them untangle their own thoughts and feelings.

Whichever meaning you are working with, you will have to be respectful and tentative when trying to clarify.

The three activities, summarising, focusing and clarifying, when used with reflection to communicate with the client, can build up to a powerful experience which in itself can enable clients to sort out problems. For some it is the end point of counselling. It can go something like this:

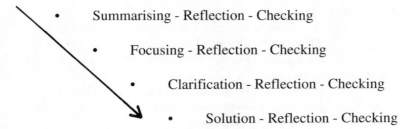

- Basic Reflection - Checking

  - Summarising - Reflection - Checking

    - Focusing - Reflection - Checking

      - Clarification - Reflection - Checking

        - Solution - Reflection - Checking

Checking is simply checking that your reflections are accurately tracking the client's thoughts and feelings. Of course, the counselling process is not always this simple, but it can be occasionally, especially over the phone, since people often phone up with the expectation of getting things sorted in double-quick time. Strong expectations can turn into self fulfilling prophesies.

The final point about this 'empathy repertoire' is that in face-to-face counselling, new counsellors often feel that their brain is about to burst trying to listen to the client whilst remembering what they've just said, preparing a summary in their head, wondering what the key issues might be and then...oh no, it's gone! They've forgotten what the client's been saying. Here the phone comes into its own and delivers one of its great advantages to you. You can make notes! Making notes can be a boon when using the phone, but don't let it take over so that you can't pay attention to what your client is saying. Brief memory aids are fine, don't start taking verbatim notes or you'll find yourself muttering 'Hang on, I haven't got that down yet!' And, of course, don't forget to destroy them at the end of the session.

Communicating genuineness

When it comes to genuineness or 'congruence' as Carl Rogers called it, many counselling texts offer a general description or definition of the activity from the client's point of view:

> 'It has been found that personal change is facilitated when the psychotherapist is what he is, when in the relationship with his client he is genuine and without 'front' or facade, openly being the feelings and attitudes which at that moment are flowing in him.'
>
> C Rogers (1961) On Becoming a Person, p 61. Constable.

Or from the counsellor's point of view:

> 'I have come to recognise that being trustworthy does not demand that I be rigidly consistent but that I be dependably real. The term 'congruent' is one I have used to describe the way I would like to be. By this I mean that whatever feeling or attitude I am experiencing would be matched by my awareness of that attitude. When this is true, then I am a unified or integrated person in that moment, and hence I can be whatever I deeply am.'
>
> C Rogers (1961) On Becoming a Person, p50. Constable.

Genuineness, then is any tangible expression of the counsellor's capacity to be in touch with her/his feelings, thoughts and bodily sensations as s/he seeks to understand the client's world of experience.

Moving from the general to the specific proves more difficult and examples are rarely quoted since the meaningful qualities of genuineness can only really be appreciated through personal experience. This is not a cop-out position since it is in the training situation where you will be provided with many moments which can be used by an experienced trainer to illustrate genuineness. In practice, genuineness raises itself as an issue in almost all counselling sessions.

The following are presented as thought-provoking items, around which you might construct a better understanding of genuineness. How many of these statements do you worry about (or maybe you recognise some from your work with clients).

1 • 'What did the client say just then? I was distracted by that noise outside the window rather than paying attention to what she was saying.'
2 • 'I don't like this person. How can I work with them when I don't like them?'
3 • 'I seem to be getting dragged into this person's problem and becoming part of it.'
4 • 'I am so bored with this session, I can hardly keep my eyes open let alone my mind on what he's saying!'
5 • 'I feel manipulated by this client into saying something I don't want to say.'
6 • 'I just can't understand what this client is talking about.'
7 • 'Aha! The client has just described exactly what happened to me years ago. I remember feeling exactly the same!
8 • 'Damn! She's hung up on me again. I get mad when she does that!
9 • 'Oh dear, this seat is uncomfortable. I can't think straight my back is killing me!'
10 • 'Wow, what a sexy voice, I really fancy him/her!'

What should you do if you are stuck in one of these situations?
    • Acknowledge the feelings you are having.
    • Decide whether the feelings are roughly:
    i) because of something in you (eg 1,2,9 or 10)
    ii) brought on by something the client has done/said (eg 5 or 8)
    iii) a mixture of your feelings and the client's behaviour (eg 4, 6 or 7)

• If you are fairly certain that the feelings are coming only from you then *don't act on them in the session*. You will need to talk to another person (your supervisor) about your feelings or emotional involvement in the client's problem. If it's a real burning issue, you may need some spot support from a colleague. (See Chapters 8 & 9). Number 9 is the exception here. If you are uncomfortable, get comfortable. You can usually do this without the client knowing when on the telephone. If you have to lose concentration for a moment, tell the client what you are doing:

> *'I'm going to have to change this chair for a different one - it's so uncomfortable I can't pay proper attention to what you are saying.'*

• Not acting on your feelings in the session would, under most circumstances, be the right course of action to take for number 6 on the above list as well. The experience and feelings you had all those years ago are *yours*, not your clients and can only get in the way of you being accurately empathic. You must try to 'clear the decks' so that you can see your client clearly and understand *their* experience, not the echoes of your own.

• If you think that your feelings are due mostly to the client's behaviour then share your feelings with the client. Be honest with a little tenderness. Introduce your feelings by saying that the feelings are yours and explain what it was that the client did that they seem to be linked to. The purpose of doing this is to offer the core condition of genuineness and it may well also be useful feedback to the client about the likely effects of his/her behaviour.

• If you think that your feelings are a mixture of your mood or temperament and the client's behaviour, say so. Be tentative and introduce the issue by saying:

> *'I'm not sure why, but I'm beginning to feel bored by what you're saying. I wonder why that is - do you think you're lacking enthusiasm for what you're saying? Does it ring any bells for you?'*

The client is then free to think about what you're saying and take it on board or dismiss it as irrelevant. They may even come back to it later.

• Number 10 is a special case for several reasons:

Firstly it is less likely that you will be overcome with passion for a client when you are speaking to them on the telephone, than if you were counselling them face-to-face.

Secondly it is clear from the various codes of ethics and practice that sexual contact between counsellor and client is forbidden.

Thirdly, generally speaking if you are using counselling skills , it is not advisable to share feelings of sexual attraction with your client. Some clients may feel attracted to you and should this happen you may prefer to reflect their feelings back to them and seek supervision.

• When appropriate, it is important to let the client know what you're thinking and feeling in a way that adds to their experience rather than subtracts from it, and in such a way that doesn't blame the client, leave them feeling rejected, judged or threatened. This is a difficult skill to learn and once again practice with feedback is the only way to perfect this aspect of your counselling.

In Training: One way of raising awareness to the early learning which underpins our lack of constructive openness about feelings is to encourage trainees to look at the whole issue of hurting someone's feelings. Use experiences in the group to highlight this.

Method:
• Split into threes and ask trainees to remember:
i) the last time they were bored with what was going on in the group (but didn't say anything),
ii) the last time they were angry with someone in the group (but didn't say anything),
iii) the last time they felt attracted to someone in the group (but didn't say anything).
• Then ask them to:
i) remember how they dealt with the feelings,
ii) share in their group of three and
   a) discuss how working on the telephone might affect how
   they deal with these feelings, then
   b) discuss ways of expressing their feelings without
   threatening or blaming the other person,
iii) try role playing or practising dealing with some awkward situations. Make some of the role plays 'unsighted'. Some tutors could step in to model their own preferred ways of handling such situations.

Communicating non-judgemental warmth.

It sometimes strikes me that most people who offer themselves for training in counselling skills must have a basic level of non-judgemental warmth. I have never yet met a truly cold person in a counselling skills training group. I hope I am not deluding myself and that counsellors are all really like the infamous mythical children's entertainer who hates children.

Even so, it is still a good thing to spend some time raising awareness about non-judgemental warmth. There are two components to the core condition of *acceptance* or non-judgemental warmth; firstly the absence of judgement and secondly the communication of warmth. It is not unusual to find yourself getting concerned about the non-judgemental bit of this core condition, since you may quickly realise the potential areas of conflict between being non-judgemental and being genuine.

You may be tempted to think that because you are working on the telephone, you cannot be seen and therefore can 'hide' your judgemental attitudes from the client. Therefore you don't need to do any work on yourself because it isn't needed.

Firstly, clients are *at least* as sensitive to non-verbal cues over the phone as counsellors.

Secondly, many clients are *super sensitive* to being judged and will react to the slightest hint of potential judgement from you.

Thirdly, self-development is a Good Thing. Don't run away from it. It scares me too, but I know that I'll be a useless counsellor if I don't give my best effort in coming to terms with the pain and joy of getting to know myself better.

It may be necessary to spend some time helping ourselves unravel the facts, fantasies and feelings around judgement. In Chapter 5 I mentioned the *johari window* as a way of understanding self-awareness and personal development. The issues surrounding judgement in our lives are best tackled by using the powerful joint action of self-disclosure and feedback from others. In training this is best achieved through exploring our attitudes to sensitive moral issues in personal development sessions, and receiving feedback from others about how we come across in general and when counselling clients.

In Training: It is sometimes necessary to raise some sensitive issues deliberately if none come up in the normal course of events during a training programme (e.g.your own moral dilemmas) to start discussion in the group.

Method:

• Sometimes it feels safer for participants to split up into twos or threes for this.

• The characteristics to facilitate are openness, flexibility and willingness to challenge and be challenged constructively without blaming.

• The sorts of issues that are well-known no-go areas for 'polite' discussion are the ones which we will have to face as counsellors. Try testing trainees feelings about some of the following:

- •Abortion
- •Violence in general
- •Rape and male violence
- •Explicit sexual talk
- •Racism - are you racist?
- •Pre/extra marital sex
- •Suicide
- •Contraception
- •Helping the police
- •Sexism - are you sexist?
- •Swearing, blasphemy and bad language
- •Gay/lesbian love, or sexual contact between people of the same sex - are you homophobic?

Learning Points:

• Be prepared for strong opinions and strong feelings. Trainees that are offended or overly 'rattled' by such a vigorous exchange may not be suitable for telephone work, since they will encounter much more robust talk on the lines.

It is practically certain that you will be confronted by a number of the issues in the training panel above in your role as a telephone counsellor even though you may have been successful in avoiding them in your life up to now. As a telephone counsellor you will have to be flexible, understanding and accepting of other people. If you are rigid and inflexible, not only will your clients not be helped by you, you yourself will also have a hard time. since in nature rigid, inflexible things tend to snap and break under pressure.

Most of the cues used in the communication of warmth involve voice quality, so it is particularly important to concentrate on warmth in the voice for people who will be working on the telephone. Once again the best help you can get here is feedback from others on what you sound like when counselling. One of the best ways of doing this is to tape-record some practice sessions with fellow counsellors or trainees and play these back in small groups or just to yourself. What do you sound like? (Yes, I know it can be a shock for many people when they hear their voice on tape. Instead of a deep, reassuring, manly drawl, I hear my thin Brummie whine!)

- How do you and your colleagues rate your voice on warmth and why?
- What characteristics of your voice would you want to change?
- What qualities of the voices of others do you admire?

In Training: Introduce the concept of non-judgemental warmth with this or a similar exercise.
Method:
- Split the group into pairs then ask trainees to think of a person in their lives with whom they associate 'warmth'. This person would be someone who has given them warmth and might even be the epitome of warmth for them.
- What qualities does this person have, what is it about them that communicates warmth?
- Then think of a person who is the exact opposite of warmth, the antithesis of warmth.
- What qualities does this 'anti-warmth' person have? How do they communicate 'anti-warmth'?
- Share in pairs, then after forming a mental picture of each person (warmth and anti-warmth) think of two key words that they associate with each person.
- Collate key words and share in large group.

Stage 2 and 3 skills
You may be wondering why the Stage 2 and 3 skills have been unceremoniously lumped together and squashed into a few lines at the end of the chapter. To refresh your memory, here is a re-run of them as they were earlier in the chapter:
Stage 2
Understanding: Helping the client see their situation with new understanding, from different perspectives, with alternative information.
Skills: All of Stage 1 skills plus summarising, linking and integrating issues into themes, offering new perspectives, sharing, challenging, immediacy (looking at what's happening right here and now between you and the client) and goal setting.

Stage 3
Action: Looking with the client at possible ways of acting in this situation. Assessing risks and possible outcomes. Helping the client evaluate the effectiveness of their new behaviour.
Skills: All of the skills of Stages 1 and 2 plus brainstorming, creative thinking, planning, implementing and evaluating plans.

If you wish to pursue Egan's model, you will find that once a relationship is established, whether on the telephone or face-to-face, these Stage 2 and 3 skills follow on naturally; the telephone neither adds nor takes away from these skills. The real effects of the phone are limited to those relationship building skills we find in Egan's Stage 1, which are the same as Carl Rogers' three core conditions of empathy, acceptance and genuineness. If you prefer not to use Egan's model, then the core conditions of empathy, congruence and acceptance that we have covered will be sufficient. If you can successfully build a helping relationship over the phone by putting the three core conditions in place, you will have created an excellent stage on which to perform Stage 2 and 3 skills. Neither you nor your client will be hindered by the phone. It will have become 'second nature'.

A Personal Account of Working on a Telephone Helpline
by Frances Mc Donnell

My involvement with telephone counselling began when I was approached by the co-ordinator of the voluntary agency I worked for to be a helpline listener/counsellor on a telephone helpline, the theme of which was the death of a partner. As a worker within this agency I interviewed and listened to women talk about the difficulties they experienced in their lives. The difficulties were many and varied and often very distressing. At this point in my career I had completed a Certificate in Counselling and was well on the way to completing a Diploma in Counselling.

Around a week after contacting the helpline organisers, I received a comprehensive pack of literature about the helpline. This included background information on the television programme the helpline was to follow. The time and date of the pre-briefing meeting, the times when the lines would be open to receive calls, and the support available to workers during and after the helpline. I learnt we would all get a free taxi ride home if we did not have transport. I was reassured by this information, the whole thing seemed well thought through, well organised and professional. I felt exited by the opportunity to work on something like this, which for me was a new and challenging experience.

The shift I was working on lasted for 4 hours. It was due to start at 9 pm and finish at 1am. Being an anxious person by nature I arrived much earlier than was strictly necessary. I decided that arriving early would give me the time I needed to orientate myself to the environment within which I was going to work. On arrival I was warmly greeted by the organizers, offered a drink and asked to wait in the reception area of the large room where the helpline was to be run. As I settled myself down into the sofa provided, I had a sense of relief at having arrived and was able to relax whilst taking in the atmosphere. I watched with interest as the room became vibrant with frenetic activity. Room dividers, tables, chairs, telephones, cables and directories were moved about with dexterity and precision. Everything had its place and what had seemed chaotic one minute, was orderly the next. The phones were connected and the system was pronounced ready for use. I was impressed.

As I observed this transformation other helpline workers arrived. Some were obviously familiar with the set up and known by the organizers. Others like me seemed tentative and nervous. As our numbers swelled to ten in total one of the organisers came to sit with us and chatted about the evening's format. Trays of freshly made sandwiches were delivered for our breaks. We were shown the drinks machine and of equal importance the location of the toilets. I found these greeting rituals resulted in my feeling more comfortable and also more part of a team and, as I discovered after the preliminary introductions, part of a team whose members came from diverse backgrounds and with varied levels of experience and knowledge.

Following the initial introductions we were reminded of the preliminary information we received relating to the television programme's content. We were then shown the programme. This focused on the experiences of a few women and their loss, through death, of a partner. The interviews were very moving and sensitive and I felt touched by the sadness and honesty of the women. We talked about the programme afterwards and all agreed that we could be in for quite an evening. I found discussing the issues relating to an individual's experience of grief and listening to the other workers ways of dealing with this both interesting and informative. I had never used my counselling skills for counselling a client by phone before so I listened intently to those who had knowledge to share.

A counsellor had been provided for the evening, not only for emotional support but also for more formal supervision. We had access to her whenever we felt the need to off-load and a room had been made available for extra privacy.

I felt well supported but also apprehensive as I took my place at one of the telephone positions. The head sets were easy to wear and meant we did not have to hold a phone to our ear, which was what I had imagined. The screens provided some privacy for each worker, and within reach we had tissues, pens, paper and a resource manual. When each of us were settled in our positions we were briefly talked through the contents of the resource manual. This included, where available, the address and telephone numbers of national and local agencies individuals could ring for support. It seemed a comprehensive list There were a number of other resource books available for making referrals and the organizers were on hand to answer any queries.

As the time for opening the lines drew near I sat and collected my thoughts in quiet and stillness. In the distance somewhere I could hear the programme coming to a close and knew that at the end a number would be given for people to ring if they needed to talk. I was one of the people waiting to listen. But what would they expect of me? I heard the helpline organizer counting down to the launch of the helpline and then nothing. Everybody seemed to be on pause. I can only guess viewers of the programme were trying to find a pen to write down the number. The first phone in the room rang and was answered, then the next and the next until it was my turn. 'Hello helpline, can I help you?'

From then on the calls came thick and fast. They were not only from individuals who had lost partners but also from those who had lost friends, children, and parents and had been reminded of their loss through seeing the programme.

Thinking about those calls reminds me of the immense sadness that was around for many of the workers that evening. I also remember, however, my relief and real sense of achievement at completing my first helpline session. The calls had been draining and I needed to have some supervision to help me through my shift and a particularly distressing call. But I had felt very connected to the callers I talked with.

I discovered that telephone counselling is different from face- to- face counselling in that my focus of awareness was much more on what I could hear rather than see. I was amazed just how much I could pick up about a person's experiencing from their voice. The intonation of the words, the trembling voice and the silences which were full of meaning. The way in which I used my counselling skills, however, were similar. Staying with the client in their world by reflecting and paraphrasing what they said, and checking out whether I had understood them correctly remained the same. I enjoyed my first experience as a helpline worker. Not only did it help me learn to trust my own counselling skills in testing circumstances, but it also gave me the experience of working closely as part of a team, being able to support others and to be supported.

7 Calls We Would Rather Not Receive

In the first edition of this book this chapter was entitled 'Problem Calls'. In subsequent workshops I began to realise that there was no such thing as a *problem* call as such, simply different degrees of calls that we would rather not receive. This catch-all category covers all manner of calls from the mildly irritating to the downright terrifying, and can be looked at from both an individual and an agency point of view. The decisions that lie behind calls we would rather not receive might be made on the basis of personal comfort or safety on the one hand, or on the basis of agency policy on the other.

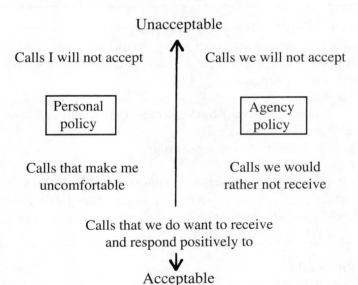

Unacceptable

Calls I will not accept ↑ Calls we will not accept

| Personal | | Agency |
| policy | | policy |

Calls that make me uncomfortable   Calls we would rather not receive

Calls that we do want to receive
and respond positively to
↓
Acceptable

We are likely to think that any call that falls into the 'personally unacceptable' category or 'unacceptable to the agency' category is a *problem call*. What we mean to say is that the call gives *us* a problem. They make us mildly uncomfortable or we might want to slam the phone down in disgust. It might be agency policy that we do not respond to certain categories of calls or caller, e.g. telephone masturbators.

In our distress at receiving calls we'd rather not have, we must be careful that we don't muddle the two categories:
  • Agency policy needs to be a mindful, considered position regarding the nature of the service and how best to use the telephone workers' skills to help the callers we wish to target.
  • Personal policy need be anything but considered. It is our 'natural' untutored response to offence.
Whilst we will not be expected to change our values, we might be expected to increase or adjust the range of issues, calls and types of caller that we are able to tolerate. This process begins with self-awareness.

In training: We usually don't know what we will find offensive until we think hard about it, or maybe not even until it happens. This gives trainees a chance to talk about those calls that worry them most.
Method:
• Ask trainees to brainstorm calls that they would *definitely* not accept (in threes).
• Collate and discuss in large group.
Learning Point:
• If appropriate at this stage, compare the trainees ideas with agency policy. Policy will need to be introduced, explained and discussed, so allow sufficient time to answer questions.

Problem calls?
We can, however, learn something from the notion of the 'problem call'. Back in 1972 when I first sat down in front of the telephone as a 'telephone counsellor' it seemed to me as though every call was a problem call. In many ways this was a very healthy frame of mind and one that it will pay you to maintain when counselling or using counselling skills on the telephone. Complacency is at worst

dangerous and at best means that your clients are not getting the most you can offer.

After a few calls however, it may become clear that some calls are more problematic than others. This is not to say that you will stop hearing all clients as unique individuals, it's just that some situations will recur and you may well wish to develop some helpful strategies so that you don't have to keep 're-inventing the wheel' every time the telephone rings. This chapter will show you some of the more common situations which cause heart searching and head scratching at telephone counselling agencies all over the country.

I'd like to start with a reminder regarding problem calls on the telephone. In Chapter 1 of this book I asked 'The Most Useful Question'. Whenever you feel stuck or stumped by circumstances ask yourself, and those around you if there's anyone there:
What would I do in this situation if it were face-to-face?

On many occasions, the answer will become clear either at this point, or after a bit of thought or discussion. I also believe that the very best answers will come from yourselves, taking into account your own, your agencies and your clients' circumstances, personalities, foibles and needs. Don't be afraid of inventing your own wheels! I've taken four types of call which I have seen cause problems in the past, both for myself and others, and offer a few pointers which I hope will help you and your clients.

Silent calls
In my view, there are three types of silent 'events' in telephone work:
• *Silences*: pauses in reciprocal conversation of varying length in a call when the caller does not speak;
• *Silent Calls*: a call which begins with silence at the caller's end and continues in silence at the caller's end for a varying length of time until either you (if agency policy permits) or the caller ends the call;
• *Silent Endings*: when after a call of varying length in which the caller has spoken, the caller falls silent and remains so for a varying length of time until either you (if agency policy permits) or the caller ends the call.

All three types of silence can last for seconds, minutes or even in very rare and extreme cases (and depending upon your agency policy) for hours.

In Training: Many trainees are worried about the prospect of receiving silent calls. An important step is to put yourself in the caller's shoes.
Method:
• Split into small groups and ask the question
'What might be happening on the other end of the phone when the caller is silent?'
• What explanations can you come up with? Share and discuss.

Face-to-face counsellors may have noticed something strange here. The term 'silence' as used above clearly doesn't mean *silence* in the face-to-face sense. In face-to-face counselling the term 'silence' means a period during the interview in which *neither* the client *nor* the counsellor speaks. I am using the term 'silence' to mean a period during which the client or caller doesn't speak. This means that one of the golden(ish) rules of counselling which all new counsellors pick up and beat themselves with, i.e. *thou shalt not interrupt a silence*, is thrown out of the window.

The two prime objectives of the counsellor are to establish and maintain contact. These are the first two steps in forging a therapeutic relationship. When you are denied visual contact and are connected only by a telephone, the only way this can be achieved is to do so verbally. Put bluntly, you've got to talk to your client even though they may be remaining silent. This doesn't mean, though, that you should engage them in *conversation* any more than you would if you were in a face-to-face situation.

As I have mentioned before, when you lose visual contact with your client and you have a degraded sense of hearing (until telephonic engineering improves sound quality) you need to establish some

basic pieces of information for yourself:
- *Is your client still there?*
- *Why are they not speaking?*
- *How are they feeling?*
- *What are they trying to communicate to you?*
- *Can you hear anything? If yes, what?*
- *What do you make of what you can hear?*

At the same time as attending to your own requirements, you will need to establish some basic pieces of information for your client; remember they can't see you either! Such as:
- *You (the listener/counsellor) are still there.*
- *You are listening.*
- *You can hear some sounds.*
- *You care very much about what is happening.*
- *You are ready to respond in a sensitive way.*
- *You want to respect their silence as much as possible whilst maintaining contact.*

There is no great mystery surrounding these things. I have found the most simple ways are nearly always the most effective. In Chapter 6 I looked at the core conditions for counselling and one was genuineness. You may like to develop some ways of establishing contact with your client through silences in ways which are genuine for you; ways which most suit you as an individual. Personally, I have found an honest and direct approach to be the best. Try saying:

'*I'm still here.*'
'*I'm still listening.*'
'*I want to hear what you have to say, if you want to carry on.*'
'*Are you still there?*'
'*Tap the phone if you are still there.*'
'*I can hear you breathing.*'
'*It sounds as though you're crying.*'
'*I thought I heard someone come into the room, do you want to carry on talking?*'
'*It's OK to say nothing, I'll just wait until you're ready to carry on.*'
'*I'll keep reminding you that I'm still here and still listening.*'

You will find that you will have to speak reasonably frequently. Just saying, "I'm still here" once, won't do, it will sound odd and awkward. If you persevere, you will develop a good 'flow'. Try using a watch with a second hand to check how frequently you are talking (it's OK to do this during the call, your client can't see you!) Too much talk from the counsellor is just as damaging to the quality of contact as too little. Depending upon what you can hear at the other end (breathing, sobbing, chattering teeth, softly whispered mumblings, or nothing at all) I have found that saying something every 15 to 45 seconds is about right. My own timing often depends upon how I'm feeling just as much as on what's happening at the other end of the line.

In Training: Trainees might need particular work on silences before they feel confident.

Method:

• In pairs, one person closes their eyes and remains silent (the 'caller') the other person, (the 'counsellor') with a watch which counts seconds in front of them, speaks into the silence trying to make and maintain contact.

• Both members of the pair then give feedback to each other on how it felt. Discuss in the large group.

Learning Points:

• For the 'counsellor': What made you want to speak or keep quiet?

• For the 'caller': How often did you have to talk in order for you to feel comfortable?

I would like to return, for a moment, to the three types of telephone silent event. In a **Silence**, the task is to keep contact with the client. Having already established contact, you must let the client know you are still there listening and at the same time satisfy yourself that the client is still there as well. Your next task is to try and understand the silence. Don't try to interpret the silence; silences mean different things to different people and at best your 'interpretation' is a guess.

You might be able to understand the silence by thinking about what the client said last, listening to any background noises and listening to any sounds your client might be making. You could then feed this back to your client either one at a time or putting them together. In this way you can incorporate the silence into the counselling session, possibly enabling your client to work through the silence constructively. Try to listen *in* to the silence...it might be an electrical fault...is the caller collecting their thoughts?...is it an angry silence?...etc.

Silences are perfectly natural elements in human interaction, but in counselling they can be more frequent and sometimes indicate that something particular is happening for the client. The telephone makes working with these silences more difficult but if you try out some of the suggestions above, you may find them less daunting.

Silent calls: These can be much more demanding than a silence. This may be because so many of us have experienced the 'threatening' version of the silent call at home. Under such circumstances a silent call is a menacing intrusion, an invasion of our privacy and safety. No wonder we get worried when a caller remains silent after we've delivered our opening "My name is ......can I help you?' patter.

In Training: More work on 'silent events'.
Method:
• Ask the group to reflect upon experiences of threatening silent calls.
• Split up into pairs to talk about the feelings involved.
Learning Points:
• Look back at the reasons generated for why people might be silent on the phone and discuss why we might feel differently about the two situations.

In a silent call, your task firstly is to make contact before you can even consider maintaining it. The first thing to do is to avoid getting hooked into the sort of feelings and behaviour you might have should you get a silent call at home. Don't say impatiently *'Who's there...I can hear you breathing...I know someone's there!!'* Try saying:

> *'Hello....is there anyone there.'*
> *'I can't hear you....I'll wait for you to start talking.'*
> *'If you are nervous just take your time...I won't hang up on you.'*
> *'Tap your phone to let me know you're there.'*
> *'I can hear you breathing/crying...I'll wait as long as you want me to.'*

As before, you may want to time yourself if the silent call lasts any appreciable time. In fact you will shortly face the most awkward problem in a silent call....*when to end the call.* How long are you prepared to (or allowed to) listen and respond to a person who is remaining silent on the other end of the phone. What has got to happen before you are convinced that they are not there any more or not interested or even asleep? I have had many callers fall asleep on the phone in the early hours, though it's not terribly difficult to recognise the familiar sounds of snoring!

If you decide that you are going to end the call, your task is to be genuine, whilst not leaving the client feeling rejected:

- Tell the caller that it's OK to be silent if that's what they want, but you have decided to end the call.
- Tell the caller why you are ending the call (there may be other callers waiting, you are tired, you need to go to the toilet, it's agency policy to limit the time of calls, etc.).
- Say that you are happy to talk to them again at any time (give your agency availability times).
- Remind them of your number.
- Give them a last chance to say something (they might even say 'Goodbye').
- Say, *'I'm putting the phone down now...Goodbye'.*

Silent endings: These have largely been covered in the section on silent calls above, but there is one difference between silent calls and silent endings. In a silent ending, you may know who the client is and you will know something of their problem since you will have been talking to them. This does change things slightly. It's almost the equivalent of a client getting up and walking out on a counsellor in the middle of an interview in a face-to-face setting. Whilst this is quite rare in a face-to-face setting, it is not so rare for a telephone counsellor to be 'left' by a client falling silent and remaining silent.

In Training: How differently do counsellors feel about silent calls and silent endings where the client's identity is known? *Method:*

• Introduce the topic of the identity of the caller to generate a general discussion on how to handle silences under different circumstances.

• Brainstorm ways of dealing with a silent ending or silent call when you know who the client is.

• Try letting different small groups look at different areas or levels, e.g. skills (what to do), emotions (how we feel), the needs of the counsellor, etc.

The techniques for dealing with silence in this situation are the same as those mentioned above. The difference is how you may feel about it. Try saying:

'Are you still there.....I don't know why you are not talking.'
'It's really difficult for me to know whether you are still there and wanting to talk.'
'I want to be here for you while you are silent, but it's difficult to know whether you want me still to be here.'
'Tap the phone if you are unable to talk but want me to hang on.'
'I will stay on the line for another two minutes before I put the phone down.'

You may feel reluctant to put the phone down on a client who you feel close to, and you may feel strong feelings of rejection if such a client puts the phone down on you. If that happens, you will have to prepare carefully for the next time you speak to them.

Abusive or threatening calls

I have already mentioned the link in some people's minds between silent calls and threatening calls. It is easy to see how this link is made in our everyday experience as phone users. This is also reinforced by films and TV drama which prey on the fantasy notion that the caller can actually see us or has some knowledge of us simply by phoning us and *remaining silent*. Of course, the caller may know some things about you such as your address and may make a guess about your gender, but other than that they are mostly in the dark.

There are two types of abusive or threatening call
1. There is the type where the caller is extremely upset or desperate and the only way they can express themselves is to get angry with the person on the other end of the phone (i.e. you!)
2. Then there is the caller who is deliberately abusive or threatening.

The difference between the two types of call is often fairly obvious when you're on the phone, but it is essential that we don't get the two muddled in this section. We may, of course, prefer to not have either type of call, but the first type is best responded to as a 'normal' call. By this I mean that we should be as empathic, respectful, accepting and congruent as usual, however rattled we might get. In most cases the caller will be able to give us enough clues about what is actually making them so angry. We need to be able to:
• Hear what they are saying - by this I mean that when people are angry their speech becomes scrambled and they can become incoherent. You may have to either ask them to speak more distinctly, without disrespectfully saying something like *'You'll have to calm down before I can hear a word you're saying'*, or, *'I find it really difficult to understand what you're saying while you're so upset,'* or weather the storm.
• Listen to the storyline - what has happened to get them so irate and abusive? There is always a reason.
• Listen to the feelings - say that you can hear that they're angry and that it may help if they can talk about it.

When the caller tells you why they are angry and abusive, it will probably be the case that they are not angry with us, the listener/

counsellor. They are actually angry with someone else or with life in general. It can be very challenging for us to continue to be non-judgemental and warm when we learn why the caller is angry, if the reason involves something we might disapprove of, e.g:

• A man says that he is angry with his wife because she feels stifled at home and wants to get a job.

• A woman is angry with her daughter because the young woman wants to terminate her pregnancy.

The second type of call is no less deserving of our empathy, etc. but it also deserves special consideration. This section is dedicated to the second type of call in the expectation that we tend to find these calls more disturbing than those from folk who have just 'flown off the handle'. We can somehow understand that life gets to us all sometimes and having a good shout at someone can be very therapeutic (even if it is the wrong person, initially!). However, it is a different kettle of fish when the caller is deliberately abusive and goes to some lengths to make it feel like a personal attack to the person receiving the call.

Sooner or later every telephone agency receives calls in which the (usually anonymous) caller threatens the listener and women seem to receive more abusive calls than men. Because we are offering a caring service where there is often the unspoken ethos *'The client is always right'*, we are often more vulnerable. We become paralysed, trapped between our need to care for the caller and our fear and revulsion at the threats made against us.

In Training: It is essential that trainees are prepared for abusive calls. Do not avoid this element of training or the difficult issues and feelings that arise.

Method:

• Check to find out how many people in the group expected to receive threatening calls. How do people feel about the prospect? Encourage trainees to share their feelings about threat and any experiences they may have had if it feels safe enough to.

• Be prepared to facilitate strong feelings, since some trainees may have personal experience of abusive calls and harassment.
• Do not outline agency policy just yet (see next training panel).
Learning Points:
• If anyone withdraws from training at this point, check with them that they are feeling OK. Follow this up with a telephone call or letter if necessary. No-one should feel blamed or be left feeling inadequate if they can't handle difficult or abusive calls.

What should we do when threatened on the phone? The first thing to do is to ask yourself *The Most Useful Question.* Then ask yourself:
  'How do I feel about abusive or threatening calls?'
  'Do I want to listen to abusive or threatening calls in general?'
And remember:
  You don't have to listen to anything you don't want to.

If the agency you work for has a policy which seems to insist that you listen to all calls no matter what is being said on the other end of the phone; remember, you don't have to work for that agency. It's OK to look after yourself. In general it's also OK to expect agency policy to provide you with a safe and secure working environment, so it is imperative that you find out your feelings on abusive calls and then you will know what to ask for. See Chapter 5 for more on agency policy.

Of course, it's also reasonable for an agency to have the general policy that volunteers and workers should never put the phone down on a caller. If this is the case, then it is reasonable to expect them to back this policy up with adequate training and selection so that workers know what to expect, are trained to deal with it and are not made to feel a failure if they don't want to work in this way. Also, agencies with such policies should provide good, readily available support (see Chapter 9) for those occasions when counsellors feel overwhelmed by a call. This is much more likely to happen during or after an abusive or threatening call which they are required to listen to.

If your agency does *not* require you to listen to abusive or threatening calls, I would then expect your training to have prepared you to end such calls in a way which does not take away your dignity or safety and which still has the client's needs firmly in sight. It might be too threatening to try and empathise with a violently abusive caller in real life, but for the purposes of preparing yourself for such a call, you may find it helpful to remember that the client must be doing this for a reason that makes sense to them.

In Training : If your agency does not require workers to listen to abusive calls, how do you recommend they end the call? (You may, for example, tell them to put the phone down immediately without saying anything.) Do not reveal your agency policy at this stage.

Method:
• In a safe, secure group (possibly split into threes or fours) ask trainees to brainstorm ways of ending an abusive call? People will often have favourite ways of doing this when they have received such calls at home.
• Allow enough time for trainees to talk through feelings associated with violence, threat or abuse which may be brought up by this activity.
• Now introduce your agency policy and discuss in the light of trainees' thoughts and feelings.

Learning Points:
• Again, be prepared to facilitate strong feelings as trainees recount distressing experiences.

For those who have never received a threatening or abusive call, it's difficult to explain quite how frightening an experience it can be. My own early experience of such calls was to react with fleeting surprise followed quickly by a mixture of fear and anger. I felt like getting stuck in and 'sorting the caller out' in a combative fashion. I would at least want to remonstrate with the caller. How dare he (I have never personally received a *threatening* call from a woman, though I know it does happen) threaten me when I was giving my time, unpaid, to help on this counselling line! Thankfully, I was not *required* to listen to threatening calls, and over a period of time, with support from others on duty with me, I was able to put the phone down without wanting to fight, or shout at, the caller.

As soon as the phone was down, I would experience a flood of fear which would stay with me for hours sometimes, particularly if I was on duty alone (now not considered good practice!) and unable to talk it through with someone else. Abusive and threatening calls still trouble me, leaving me with sticky feelings which, although they go after a while, are much better dealt with by having good on-line support (see Chapter 8).

The one redeeming feature of a fair number of threatening calls is that the caller doesn't usually stay on the line for long. They can be fairly brief, explosive affairs. The effect is all the more shocking and the shock can take a few minutes to develop in our physiological systems, so if possible, don't take calls for at least 15 minutes after receiving a threatening call. Your body will still be dealing with the shock and you will not be able to listen effectively to the next call.

In Training: Experienced listener/counsellors will know that abusive and threatening calls, whilst not frequent, can be a common experience. If your policy is to take such calls, you have to prepare workers thoroughly to listen to the calls, engage the caller and most importantly, not get damaged by the process. This requires good training and good support systems. *Method:*

• In a safe secure group, (split into threes or fours), a good exercise to start off with is to ask trainees to write down as many unpleasant, abusive, threatening and menacing sentences as they can think of.

• Share in the whole group and write up on a flip chart. Discuss in whole group.

Learning Points:

• This book does not provide a complete training programme, just training hints and tips. If you don't know how to provide such preparation through training, employ a training consultant who does.

• Skills development and personal growth for trainees go absolutely hand in hand in this area of training. Always give enough time for trainees to talk through their feelings about threat, violence and abuse. Only use trainers who can handle this themselves.

If you do choose to listen to abusive or threatening calls you must answer the question *'Why?'* before proceeding. Some reasons might be:

> *'I am a caring person and I want to be unconditionally warm to all callers and clients regardless of their behaviour.'*
> *'I am used to being abused and insulted. It's like water off a duck's back to me.'*
> *'People are basically good and there must be a reason why this person is being abusive. If I can understand the reason, maybe counselling can help.'*
> *'It doesn't bother me. I'm not easily offended.'*
> *'I quite like being spoken to like this.'*
> *'Listening to phone threats will help my personal growth.'*

On balance my experience has shown me that people *are* basically good and that if I can provide the core conditions and the client wants to change, then counselling can help. I do not believe that people are abusive without a reason. If I can talk to them for long enough without getting too angry or frightened myself I might be able to understand what they are trying to say through their threats and abuse. Of course, that's what I *think*. What I *do* in any given situation may easily depend upon how I feel at the moment a call arrives. Whether it's because I've had an argument with my children, or

Aston Villa have lost to Birmingham City, I need to be able to 'listen' to myself and if I feel vulnerable, remind myself that *I don't have to listen to this stuff.*

Simply deciding that you don't have to put up with anything you don't want to is no protection from the shock of the unexpected. And if you do decide that you are prepared to listen to such calls, there is the small question of what to do when it happens. So what might you do when you are minding your own business, the phone rings and the caller says *'I know where you live and I'm going to fucking slit your fucking throat you bastard!'*

If you decide to take the call the first thing to do is *listen very carefully.*

Don't worry, you won't get 'drawn into' the caller's world of violent threats or 'infected' by their violence. Most people, quite sensibly, 'close down' to abusive calls so that they can't hear the horrible things the caller is saying. This natural reaction, whilst understandable, will not help the caller. Do the exact opposite of closing down; turn up an imaginary volume control in your head so that you catch all of the subtle nuances in the caller's speech. This will have two effects:
  1. If you are surprised, shocked, frightened or nervous it will help get rid of your immediate nerves, giving you something to concentrate on.
  2. It will reveal a richness of detail in the 'standard abuse' which will give you the opportunity to understand more about the caller's world and feed back more to him/her. It will help you hear the caller as a unique individual, something it's very difficult to do when they're being verbally threatening, abusive and violent.

Then in the middle of it all, try to *remember your task is to offer the core conditions.* It's easy to forget this in the heat of the moment, so remind yourself - Empathy, Warmth and Genuineness. At the same time, remember you're not there just to be the passive butt of someone else's bile:
Empathy means we will try to listen, to find meaning in the client's abuse, to try to put ourselves in their world.

Warm acceptance means that we are accepting them as a human being, not condoning their behaviour.
Genuineness means that we are still a human being ourselves and we are not there to be the limp victim of someone else's abuse.

In Training: Try presenting the trainees with some abusive, threatening language.
Method:
• It's sometimes too much to expect people to both say and listen to abusive language in the same exercise, so make a tape of yourself or another trainer saying some threatening or violent things.
• Split up into threes, tell the groups that they can hold hands if they wish, for some extra support.
• Play the tape to the whole group, sitting in threes.
• Talk about responses and feelings in the threes then discuss in large group.
Learning Points:
• This exercise is similar to the training panel on p 120, but there the learning is to become aware of the *meaning* of the abusive language for each trainee. Here the idea is to see *how it feels* to be 'hit between the ears' with abusive language.

Exactly how you strive to be genuine, empathic and non-judgementally warm under these trying circumstances will depend upon what your agency offers, your personality, how you feel at the time and what the caller is saying.

Common ground?
Abusive or threatening calls are, for many people, linked with calls from telephone masturbators, see below. This link can be a personal, theoretical or political one:
> • *Personal*: to receive either type of call is very unpleasant indeed and can leave you feeling invaded, abused, conned, duped, or even raped. A call from a man wanting you to talk about your body and sexual preferences whilst he masturbates would be

extremely threatening to most people.

• *Theoretical*: both kinds of call fall into the same category of event for many people, i.e. a distorted expression of the need to dominate others through humiliating them. This view may well lead to ideas about how to respond to such callers.

• *Political*: both types of call are further evidence of male violence since the vast majority of these calls are made by men. After listening to a few from men and even fewer from women, there is, in my experience, a different quality to the calls made by women. This could, however, be due to my inability to step outside my standard perceptions and responses in terms of heterosexual, gender-based stereotypes.

There is the view that this behaviour is a 'cry for help'. Whether you hold that view or not, such abusive, or overtly sexually involving, behaviour when expressed over the telephone is certainly a piece of human communication. All communications are made with the expectation of a response and I believe that my responsibility as a counsellor is to give a response that:

• is as free as possible from the clutter of my own fears;
• is as clear and unequivocal as I can make it;
• adds to the client's experience rather than takes away from it;
• leaves the client feeling that s/he has encountered a real person with real feelings;
• does not leave the client feeling that their behaviour is either approved of or disapproved of;
• does not reject the client as a worthless person.

The above holds true whether or not I decide to listen to the call. Even if I decide to not listen, I would like to put the phone down in a manner congruent with the above aspirations. In other words, in the very act of not listening and putting the phone down I will be trying to offer the core conditions of empathy, warmth and genuineness. If I decide to listen to the call, I've somehow got to deliver the core conditions for the duration of a call in which the caller is trying to involve me in their sexual fantasies, either directly or indirectly.

Whatever your view, if you do make a link between abusive, threatening calls and those made by telephone masturbators, you may well decide that a similar response is required for all such calls. I think that a common set of principles applies to all calls and that the type of call is largely immaterial. I hope that view comes over clearly as you read through this book. However, I feel strongly about the element of personal choice here. As a counsellor I am not obliged to listen to anything I don't want to. I am not expected to make a personal growth issue out of this either, I won't try to tackle it just because it's there. And I do not have to apologise to anyone for my views or decisions.

In Training: Provide plenty of opportunity to talk this whole issue through. Many views will be represented in the training group and there must be enough of the right quality time and space to give everyone who wants, a chance to talk.
Learning Points:
• If anyone withdraws from training at this point, do follow them up with a call or letter, offering them a chance to talk and either withdraw or re-join the training without feeling a failure. (This should also happen if anyone withdraws at any time for any reason.)

Telephone masturbators
When I first volunteered to work on a telephone counselling line, I never imagined that people might phone up and want to listen to someone talking to them whilst they masturbated. Maybe it came as a shock to you too? It didn't take me too long to get used to the idea in theory, since I also believed that only women would be prey to telephone masturbators. I was wrong.

It is true to say that the majority of callers wanting to say or listen to sexually explicit language whilst masturbating require a female to take part, a small minority either want a man or don't care who they talk to. Most callers wanting this are men, though I was completely taken by surprise by a caller purporting to be a woman on one occasion a few years ago.

To those who are familiar with this type of call, there are some distinct types, sharing common features:

- Some callers are excited by the element of surprise or deceit. They appear to want to 'con' the listener, engaging you in sexually explicit conversation without letting you know that they're masturbating. They never let the language get crude enough to betray their activity and they try to conceal their climax.
- Other callers are crude from a very early point in the call, asking blunt personal questions about clothing, parts of the body and sexual preferences - what colour knickers have you got on, are your tits big and do you like to suck big cocks? These callers may not try to conceal their masturbating or their climax.
- As mentioned above, some callers use directly violent, abusive and threatening language.

(Incidentally, if you are shocked by the language I've just used, then it will be a useful starting point for you, since you will almost definitely hear much stronger language when on duty.)

Ten years ago the problem of telephone masturbators was high on the list of priorities in training for telephone counselling agencies. Since then we have seen the advent of telephone 'chatlines' (some offering explicit sexual dialogue popularly known as 'sexlines') and they do provide a service which has taken the pressure off telephone counselling agencies to some extent in some regions. Callers who are 'upfront' about their sexual demands in a telephone conversation may now be more likely to phone a chatline where they can guarantee finding someone who will play along and indulge their fantasies.

Explicit talk, and particularly offering a service which is deliberately orientated towards masturbation, is not condoned by telephone service providers and may be judged obscene. However, although such chatlines are monitored to keep them within the guidelines, I believe that in reality, most callers' needs are likely to be met.

The issues surrounding how to deal with telephone masturbators are practically guaranteed to cause feelings to run high. One way or another people will react strongly to the prospect of receiving such a call. Some people are so shocked and outraged that they refuse point blank to talk about it or even think about it. These strong views and feelings reflect the strong reactions felt by counsellors when they receive such calls. Outrage, shock, abuse, violation of self and downright anger are all common reactions, however experienced the counsellor might be. These strong feelings are the starting point to help us decide whether we are going to listen to these calls or put the phone down as soon as we realise what's going on.

In Training: The following information is given earlier in this chapter when dealing with abusive and threatening calls:
• Experienced telephone counsellors will know that calls from persons seeking sexual gratification whilst not frequent, can be a common experience. Workers must be prepared for this and the first step is to help them decide if they want to listen to this type of call.
• If your policy is to take such calls, you have to prepare workers thoroughly to listen to the calls, engage the caller and most importantly, not get damaged by the process. This requires good training and good support systems.
Method:
• In a safe secure group (e.g. split into threes). A good exercise to start off with is to ask trainees to write down as many sexually explicit sentences as they can think of.
• Share in the whole group and write up on a flip chart, then discuss in whole group.
• Then in pairs, explore feelings about these calls, each partner should help the other to approach a decision.
• Reconvene large group, share what it felt like.
Learning Points:
• Skills development and personal growth for trainees go absolutely hand in hand in this area of training. Always give enough time for trainees to talk through their feelings about sexual violence Only use trainers who can handle this themselves.

If you do choose to listen to calls from people wanting sexual gratification you must answer the question *'Why should I respond?'* or, *'Why do I want to respond?'* before proceeding. Some reasons might be:

- *'I am a caring person and I want to be unconditionally warm to all callers and clients regardless of their behaviour.'*
- *'I am used to this kind of language. It's like water off a duck's back to me.'*
- *'I get really turned on by explicit sexual language, so I'm going to be disappointed if I don't get some calls like this.'*
- *'People are basically good and there must be a reason why this person is behaving like this. If I can understand the reason, maybe counselling can help.'*
- *'It doesn't bother me. I'm not easily offended.'*
- *'However perverted these desires are, they must talk them through with someone.'*
- *'I quite like being spoken to like this.'*
- *'Listening to explicit sexual demands will help my personal growth.'*
- *'Men need to get relief somehow and I'd rather they phoned up like this than go out and rape someone.'*

Just reading these questions will start you thinking about your motives. If you answer them as honestly as possible it will help you avoid falling into the trap of using counselling work to get your own needs met at the expense of the caller.

In Training: If your agency policy is to listen to such calls or give your workers the choice, the agency must support this position with adequate preparation, support after calls and supervision. There is no substitute for practice in real life, it is a little difficult to arrange for this category of call. Role-plays are about as near as you will get to the real thing and even then you will need to take care.

Method:
- Prepare the trainees for the role play by warming up with some sexually explicit talk. Get trainees to brainstorm as

many sexually explicit words as they can. Put up on the flipchart. How did that feel?
• Ask trainees to brainstorm as many sexual acts and words for them as possible.
• Put up on flipchart. How did that feel?
• Ask trainees to volunteer for the role of caller, then split into pairs for a role play back to back. Groundrules could include the idea that the counsellor can stop or hang up anytime and help could be on hand from experienced counsellors if anyone is upset by the exercise. Role play should last 5 minutes maximum.
• Share in pairs, then de-role thoroughly. Share in large group. Check that trainees stay out of role during large group discussion.

Learning Points:
• Try the above steps 'cold' without the warm up stages. (In real-life the calls come in without warning.)
• Pay careful attention to creating an atmosphere of empathy, warmth and genuineness in the group and allow plenty of time for discussion. In any event this is good modelling of the core conditions in a counselling relationship and should be a constant aim in training.
• It should be obvious that this will be a highly challenging activity for all trainees, and trainers too unless they are experienced in running sexuality workshops.
• Be aware of how individuals or the group may discharge the embarrassment, tension, or feelings of sexual arousal by humour or changing the subject. Be prepared to facilitate this by sensitively pointing it out to the group.
• De-roling after any role play is essential, and after role plays in which strong feelings are brought up, it is absolutely crucial that all participants are given plenty of opportunity to shed their roles, and the associations and feelings attached to them. Leave plenty of time for this; do not rush it through at the end.

The suggestions I have made for training are not a recipe for success, but you may find them useful as guidelines if you have not trained workers specifically to receive abusive, threatening or sexually explicit calls before. The process can be put into a nutshell as:

• Awareness raising

• Decision making

• Skill development

Using personal development as the main vehicle throughout

A group atmosphere of warmth and trust is essential if your trainees are to experience this as a positive learning opportunity, rather than an opportunity for gratuitous sex talk or to make a political point or just to scare volunteers off! Getting the balance right may take some time, but openness on the part of the trainers goes a long way to ensuring a productive, positive, training event. Good luck!

Third party calls

• 'Hello? My friend is pregnant and doesn't know what to do. How do you get an abortion?'
•' I'm sure that my niece is being abused by my sister's new boyfriend and she's only six. Should I call the police, social services or what? Will you do it for me?'
• 'There was terrible screaming and shouting from next door half an hour ago, some loud bangs then it all went quiet. Please can you get an ambulance? I'm worried that someone's been hurt. Please call one now.'
• I'm only phoning 'cos I'm desperate. He keeps me locked up in the house all day because he thinks that if I go out some man will look at me and I'll be off. It's a stupid idea and he knows it, but ever since he had the operation he thinks I won't love him anymore. He needs help and if he doesn't get it soon I *will* be off! What can you do to help us? Someone has got to get him to go for help.'
• 'My daughter thinks that you can't get pregnant the first time you have sex. She's here now, will you tell her 'cos she won't

listen to me. (*Voice shouting away from phone*), 'Angela, will you come here *now!* There's someone on the phone who's got something you need to listen to young lady!'

All of the calls above touch onto the issue of 'third party' calls to a greater or lesser degree. A third party call is one in which the caller is seeking your involvement, or help, on behalf of a (often, but not always, anonymous) person who is not present - the third party. The key words here are 'seeking your involvement', since the experience of receiving a third party call is as close to feeling 'hooked' as you can get. Just like a fish you may feel tempted to take a bite, but beware, you may get caught and end up in a net! So great is our desire to help that sometimes we try to help where it's not been asked for by the person it most directly concerns.

This is the dilemma of a third party call. The person who seems in need isn't there and can't be asked if they are in need of help or, if truly in need, whether they want help, and if help is genuinely wanted, whether they would choose you. All of this discussion about their life is happening without their knowledge or permission, and in their absence. Even if they can be located, you will probably not know whether they are talking to you voluntarily. (It is important that the people we are trying to help are not brought to the phone under duress, as in the last vignette above.)

Whilst we are attending to the business of the third, absent person we are missing the opportunity of working with the real client. This means the caller, the one on the end of the phone. In both face-to-face and telephone counselling situations, *your client is always the person you're talking to.*

Some simple guidelines might help deal with these awkward situations:
- Ask yourself, 'Just who is the client here?' whenever you suspect you might be getting drawn into counselling a third person.
- Consult agency policy as to whether third party calls are responded to at all, e.g. you should report all cases of suspected

abuse or you should call an ambulance if you think someone's life is in danger.
• Take appropriate action to deal with the request for help if permitted by agency policy.
• Get your counselling head back on and offer the core conditions to the client at hand.

Of course these are fine words but how do you actually do it?

In Training: Make sure you have an agency policy appropriate to the needs of your target group of potential callers and within the skill limits of your telephone listener/counsellors. These third party calls are very difficult to handle well.
Method:
• Use the examples on the previous page to either:
  • generate discussion about the general issue of third party calls.
  • identify the 'real client' in each vignette.
  • get trainees to suggest ways of dealing with different types of third party calls. This could end up with developing scripted statements.
• Discuss the difficulties of dealing with the natural tendency to want to rescue and help everybody in the situation.
Learning Points:
• Introduce agency policy and explain how it works to help the real clients and the agency's target group of potential callers.

Try some of this training exercise yourself now. How would you respond to the above calls? Use the guidelines mentioned on the previous page taking note of the possible pitfalls below. Here are the calls again:

'Hello? My friend is pregnant and doesn't know what to do. How do you get an abortion.'
  • Pitfall: Don't immediately assume that the caller is really talking about herself.

'I'm sure that my niece is being abused by my sister's new boyfriend and she's only six. Should I call the police, social

services or what? Will you do it for me?'
- Pitfall: Don't start a discussion about the relative merits of police vs social services and what you would do if you were the caller.
- Pitfall: Find out what agency policy advises in such cases. Are you authorised to make such calls?

'There was terrible screaming and shouting from next door half an hour ago, some loud bangs then it all went quiet. Please can you get an ambulance? I'm worried that someone's been hurt. Please call one now.'
- Pitfall: Don't get freaked out by the thought of someone lying injured somewhere. If the caller was so concerned s/he could always dial 999 for an ambulance themselves.
- Pitfall: What does agency policy advise? Usually you will be expected to get the caller to call the emergency services themselves if you believe the report to be real. (If it is not a real incident, the emergency services will tire of receiving false alarms from your agency.)

'I'm only phoning 'cos I'm desperate. He keeps me locked up in the house all day because he thinks that if I go out some man will look at me and I'll be off. It's a stupid idea and he knows it, but ever since he had the operation he thinks I won't love him anymore. He needs help and if he doesn't get it soon I will be off! What can you do to help us? Someone has got to get him to go for help.'
- Pitfall: Don't start having a conversation about, or get involved with, the third person by asking questions to satisfy your natural curiosity like, "What was the operation he had?" etc. Your effort should be directed to the real client and their anxiety.

*'My daughter thinks that you can't get pregnant the first time you have sex. She's here now, will you tell her 'cos she won't listen to me. (*Voice shouting away from phone), *'Angela, will you come here now! There's someone on the phone who's got something you need to listen to young lady!'*
- Pitfall: Angela may already be a client of your agency and poor handling of this situation may spoil that relationship.

If, however, she is not already a client, she may well be put off any future contact and will tell her friends about her experiences too.

Throughout this exercise remember to look at the guidelines on page 131. Continuously refer to your agency policy or your own personal policy on third party calls and never forget who the real client is, namely *the person you are talking to.*

Hoax calls

Hands up if you worry about what to do if you receive a hoax call? Have you ever received one? What is your agency policy about them? Do you get more hoax calls from young people messing about? By the way, just what *is* a 'hoax call'?

Some of you reading this will be convinced that you can answer this question and you've probably spent a lot of time which you feel has been wasted listening to children giggling, burping and farting down the phone at you, or just blurting out the odd rude word or two, or remaining silent, or giving a contradictory account of their problem. To dismiss these and other types of behaviour in children and adults as 'hoaxing' may well cause you to miss the one call in ten or twenty from a person in genuine need. The child being physically or sexually abused, the adolescent on the brink of suicide through bullying, or the woman desperately trying to pluck up the courage to report a rape.

Whatever our view of the authenticity of calls, it is genuinely difficult to know how to deal with a call that beings with a robust, 'Fuck off!'. It is great if we have a catch-all category of calls we would rather not have titled *Hoax Calls* so that we can dump any that are just too difficult, irritating or perplexing to deal with. The missing word here is *initially*. Many calls may be *initially* difficult, irritating or perplexing, but the measure of our telephone skills may be in how many calls we can persevere with until the true nature of the call is revealed to us by the caller. A 'Fuck off!' may turn into almost anything from an abused and angry child to a drunken and desperate parent.

Some agencies and individuals set about the task of trying to distinguish between such valid calls and the real hoaxers. Indeed some agencies will even alert workers to well known, so-called, 'hoaxers'. Such a quest is, in my view, useless. It is based on the false premise that you can know enough about the caller from a few seconds on the phone to make an informed decision. It is further based on the incorrect view that people in distress act in a stereotypically distressed way. It is finally flawed by the assumption that a hoaxer is a person who will always, and can only, play hoaxes and never become a person in real need.

In the early sixties, the American psychologist Stanley Milgram conducted a now famous experiment in which he led volunteers to believe that they had just killed another volunteer in the experiment by giving him ever larger electric shocks until he died of a heart attack. The interesting part for me was not that the majority of ordinary people could be persuaded to electrocute a fellow human being, but how they reacted to the process of the experiment and the realisation they had killed someone. The experiment was recorded on film. What do you think they did? How would ordinary people react?

Well, they reacted in just about every way you could think of. Some cried, some exclaimed *'My god what have I done,'* or, *'Oh no, this is terrible'*. A clergyman sat in dumbfounded silence and one man laughed. He couldn't stop giggling; in the middle of the horrific situation he snorted and sniggered like a schoolboy. He giggled all the way through, shock after shock, as his volunteer partner (in the next room) screamed and begged him to stop and eventually 'died'. There could be, however, no doubt that given my view of the whole scene, I could see that the man in question was giggling through extreme distress.

There really is no way of telling how people will react to stress and our task of understanding what's actually going on for the caller is made all the more difficult because counsellors can rarely see the whole scene, especially when working on the telephone. The interesting comment on us as helpers is why, when given a partial view of the world of our client on the phone, do we have such a strong tendency to believe the worst?

If a caller is behaving in an inconsistent, contradictory or just inexplicable way, don't be too quick to label them as time wasting, manipulative or a hoaxer. Doing this is an attempt by you to make sense of their world from *your* point of view. Your task is to seek the information from *their* world of experience which will make sense of *their* behaviour.

In the vast majority of cases, people behave in a way which makes sense to them. (This does not mean to say that they are not in distress, hurt or frightened.) Some counsellors hold the view that people *always* behave in a way which makes sense to them at some level. I generally agree with this view. My task as a counsellor is to find the sense in the client's experience and then I will be able to understand them. In our book on counselling research, (Sanders and Liptrot 1993) Damian Liptrot wrote we would find a strong relationship between ice cream sales at seaside resorts and deaths by drowning. As more ice creams are sold, more people drown. We would be silly to jump to the conclusion that eating ice cream causes people to drown. Instead we must look for the hidden information, the missing evidence which helps us see the whole scene. In this case it is that as the temperature goes up, so do both ice cream sales and swimming in the sea. Now we can see how all three are linked.

This kind of detective work might sound a bit like *Mission Impossible*, but it is the very stuff of counselling and turns out to be not that difficult. It takes a little patience, respect and some non-judgemental warmth. These three qualities were missing in private eye Jake Gittes, the character played by Jack Nicholson in the film *'Chinatown'*. He confronts Evelyn Mulwray played by Faye Dunaway over the identity of a mysterious young woman, central to the plot. Mrs Mulwray's evasive behaviour and apparent deceit takes Jake Gittes to the edge of violent frustration.

'Who is she?' he asks as he shakes Evelyn.
'She's my daughter,' she answers.

More lies, thinks Jake and he slaps Evelyn across the face in frustration, hoping to get to the truth.
'She's my sister,' Evelyn gasps as Jake slaps her face the other way.
'She's my daughter.'
Slap!
My sister.'
Slap!
'My daughter. She's my sister *and* my daughter!'
Evelyn collapses, looks away from Jake and sobs.
'My father and I...Understand? Or is it too tough for you?'

Now Jake Gittes had found the clue which helped him understand the contradictory information. He had the missing piece of evidence which allowed him to see the whole scene. As counsellors, our methods may not seem as direct, but we must not let our frustration get in the way of holding all contradictions until we understand the client's world well enough for the elements within it to be no longer contradictory.

I would invite you to consider the possibility that *there is no such thing as a hoax call.*

Suicidal callers

When asked to rate calls according to their difficulty, telephone counsellors in the USA rated calls from suicidal people very difficult (Walfish 1983 - see p.170). What to do when we receive a suicidal call is by no means clear, since individuals and agencies have very different positions regarding the ethics of helping in these situations. We might, as individuals, base our helping ethics on a personal moral position, whilst the agency might base its position on the aims of the agency, cultural mores, religious views, funding requirements, statutory responsibilities, etc.

Although many people worry about the legal position, it is almost impossible to compromise your position as a helper whilst on the telephone, unless the caller specifically asks you to summon help and you refuse. The anxiety we feel in such circumstances is much more likely to come from our own fear, upset and indecision caused by our personal moral position. Whatever we think we believe, it can nearly always be thrown into confusion and conflict when someone calls threatening to kill themselves. Sometimes we get the distinct impression that the caller either will or will not carry out the treat from a 'gut reaction' or 'intuition', sometimes we believe that the caller is really asking for something else, or that the call is a 'cry for help'. Sometimes the caller convinces us that they are in the middle of an actual attempt on their life and that they want support or a friendly ear whilst they die. The main problem we, as listeners, have in these situations is the terrible feeling of helplessness, the realisation that even if we did want to do something we probably couldn't because the caller can put the phone down whenever they like.

There are two basic options as individuals and as agencies when thinking about how to plan policies to respond to suicidal callers. Neither is 'recommended' or 'preferable', it is ultimately a matter for personal choice. Do not work for an agency which requires responses that conflict with your personal position. You will not serve either your clients or yourself by compromising in this way.

The listening and accepting option
This option requires careful preparation of helper/counsellors, since we will not be able to listen and accept the caller in a respectful way if we do not feel comfortable with this option. It is not an easy option to go for, even if it is roughly in accord with our personal moral code. The skills required are no different than those outlined throughout the rest of the book, and the support necessary for helpers in this option can be considerable. Helpers, however certain of the correctness of allowing callers control over their destiny, will experience doubts and uncertainties during and after the call. Agency procedures must make provision for this.

The intervention option
Mental health professionals have developed several ways of estimating the seriousness of suicide threats in face-to face situations. Such assessments are sometimes called 'Lethality Assessments' in the USA and cognitive approaches to counselling have developed a number of techniques to reduce the likelihood of the person making

a successful attempt to kill themselves. Most assessments of this type are also based on the notion that if the suicidal person is in great danger, the helper can always restrain them or have them forcibly admitted into hospital. This does not apply to telephone work. Any lethality assessment and intervention must be sufficiently sensitive as to be essentially undetectable as a strategy, lest the caller put the phone down and break contact. This option calls for the greatest skills and finest judgement. The following model is based on the work of Neville and Barnes (1985) who integrated ideas from several sources.

The administration of this option is also crucial since it really helps if a list of suicidal callers can help identify a repeat caller and help with understanding their history of previous suicide attempts.

A. Lethality Assessment
The first task is to assess the likelihood of the caller making a successful attempt on their life. This must be done sensitively. Although you will need to collect a fair amount of information about the caller you should not ask too many questions and it is best to avoid direct questions about the caller's identity and location. This may be taken by the caller as an attempt to trace or catch them.
1. Does the caller have a plan? If yes, how likely is it to succeed? (Different methods have varying degrees of lethality, e.g. paracetamol, carbon monoxide poisoning [car exhaust], drowning, jumping, hanging and paracetamol are all high; domestic gas [excepting the risk of explosion], wrist cutting and minor tranquillisers such as librium and valium are all low.)
2. Does the caller have a history of suicide attempts? Many previous attempts gives a greater chance of success now.
3. Isolation. The more physically, socially and emotionally isolated the caller is, the more likely they are to succeed.
4. Personal resources such as supportive friends and relatives, other professional helpers, e.g. social workers, health visitors will lessen the chances of success.
5. Stressors in the current life situation of the caller will increase the chances of a serious attempt being made.
6. Situational factors also affect the likelihood of success, e.g.

weekends, holidays (Christmas), early hours of the morning are times of higher risk. Anniversaries (of separation), birthdays (of deceased) are further vulnerable times.

7. Delusional and hopeless callers are more likely to kill themselves.

B. Interventions

The first aim is to keep the caller on the phone by keeping them talking. This at least ensures that they are still alive and keeps open the possibility of successful intervention. Do everything possible to keep contact in this way.

1. Allow the caller to 'let off steam' and vent their feelings.

2. Reinforce positive statements or hopeful thoughts.

3. Avoid reflection of feelings, especially negative ones. (If the caller says 'It's hopeless, I've lost my job', don't say 'It's hopeless, you've lost your job.')

4. Identify alternative options to suicide, e.g. getting angry with someone, writing feelings in a letter, talking to people, etc.

5. Acknowledge and understand the caller's distress and desperate situation. Take them seriously. Don't try to 'call their bluff'. This is dangerous.

6. Negotiate a 'no-suicide contract' and include in this the notion that either they will call you back to let you know how they are doing, or you will call them. Keep your promises.

Along with avoiding direct questions, helpers would also do well to avoid arguing with or antagonising the caller. Be careful with challenge. Be equally careful with humour. If badly judged or perceived as sarcasm by caller it could be dangerous. Finally get plenty of support for yourself after the call and review your performance thoroughly. Keep good records should the caller contact another helper at the agency.

There is further information on dealing with suicidal callers in Chapter 10 'Research into Telephone Helping and Counselling' in the section on Suicidal Callers on pp.174-177.

Service abusers - chronic callers

However new the service, telephone helplines all have their share of repeat callers. Unless you offer a listening service specifically for such 'chronic callers', people who call regularly just for a chat, or those whom you suspect of calling repeatedly using different personae can be either a slight nuisance or a someone who is abusing your service to the detriment of other callers wishing to get through. How such callers are handled depends upon the aims and policy of the agency. Whatever procedures result from this should be clearly identified and all helpers thoroughly prepared for appropriate responses.

Heywood (1980) has identified three kinds of repeat callers that helpers and agencies will need to distinguish between in order to develop an effective policy, namely masturbators, hesitant, silent or lonely callers and mentally ill callers. Tarran (1982) added a category of caller who abuses the service for no apparent reason termed the 'General Service Abuser' or GSA. It may be useful for agencies and individuals to undertake their own categorisation project to help them understand the policy developments best suited to their situation. Local conditions will determine the nature of the calls received and will also help shape policy. The following steps might help:

- Review call types over the past year. If statistics are not available, ask volunteers to estimate the call types and volumes.
- Categorise in terms of chronic callers, starting with the categories listed above and adapting them to suit your needs.
- Decide how you want to respond to each category of caller; will you listen to masturbators? Does the local community mental health team run a good drop-in service and helpline, obviating the need for you to respond to such callers or act as a referral service? Do you want your lines clogged up with lonely callers whilst the potential callers you are targeting wait?
- Write your policy and procedures carefully around these decisions, clearly stating what volunteers are supposed to do when they receive each type of call.
- Ask volunteers for feedback before amending your procedures prior to issue.

Agencies should have policy and procedures for each category of caller, with the most extreme response being to terminate the call immediately upon identification of the call. There are no right or wrong policies or procedures, simply those which will serve your target callers best. Policy should have two main steps:

• Identification of call type. Ask volunteers/workers for help here, their experience will be invaluable and up-to-the-minute. Look out for the following signs of chronic callers:
  • Caller says they call often.
  • Caller asks for helper's name or other personal details.
  • Caller identifies other helpers at agency.
  • Caller says ' I wasn't expecting you,' or 'You're a new voice.'
  • Caller tries to steer conversation in a particular direction, e.g. sexual or political.
  • Caller spins out conversation by any device.
• Procedure for dealing with the call. Each category should be different, but the following general guidelines might be helpful:
  • Keep a list of suspected chronic callers.
  • Log all calls plus the client identification (a code number or name is sufficient).
  • Set a time limit for the call. Don't make excuses, simply explain that the caller has called several times with the same problem and that the service needs to be available for other callers.
  • Do not encourage the caller to call back.
  • Find out if they have any other means of support or company. Suggest they use such support.
  • Try to make a referral to another agency, not to 'pass the buck', but to get genuine treatment.

Remember that chronic callers deserve respectful treatment. Even though they may be a lonely chronic caller today, a family bereavement, being the victim of a crime or some other crisis could bring them to your agency as one of your targeted callers tomorrow. Ensure that your handling of chronic callers has not already put them off by offhand or disrespectful treatment.

8 After the Call

The very first call I ever took (at the age of 20, after twelve weeks 'training') was from a caller who mistook the counselling service where I worked as a volunteer, for Dial-a-Prayer. After some initial confusion on both our parts it turned out that the caller had a terminal illness causing great pain, had had both legs amputated and to cap it all her husband had recently died. She had taken what she hoped was an overdose of barbiturate sleeping pills and wanted a kind voice to read prayers to her as she slipped away.

We talked for a while after which she asked if I would read the Bible to her. My first dilemma was that since I am not a Christian, I had to decide whether I felt comfortable reading from the Bible, and whether she would feel comfortable with me reading from the Bible. I explained my dilemma and together we decided that it would be OK for me to do it. After a frantic search of the office and a stroke of luck, we were able to find a copy and I read some of her favourite passages to her until my asking her what I should read next got no reply. She would not tell me her telephone number nor where she lived. She told me only her first name and that she thought that it was time for her to be with her husband.

After listening intently for any signs of life at the other end of the phone I turned to the other counsellor on duty with me, (he was a catholic priest and had gathered that something unusual was happening from my anguished expressions and the 'Bible hunt'). He pointed to the chair on which I was sitting and as I looked down I saw the trousers I was wearing were literally soaked in sweat. It looked as if I had wet myself. I wasn't quite sure what I was feeling. I didn't know what to do next. I gave a quick nervous laugh and then cried in his arms for what seemed like hours. The training course had not prepared me for this.

I had learned how important it is that counsellors have access to support whenever they want it, whatever their working situation.

In Training: Although the issue here is support, it is a good idea to acknowledge that agency policy can be supportive in providing good boundaries in the form of dos and don'ts in such distressing situations.

Method:

• Try presenting this scenario as a case study and asking trainees to debate the professional/agency policy issues involved.

  • What would *they* do in this situation?
  • What do they think it is *correct* to do?

• Try asking the following questions:

  • Does my agency policy support me in my decision to listen and talk to an apparently dying woman?
  • Should I have called the police, ambulance or asked for assistance?
  • Should I have tried to persuade her to tell me her address so that I could rescue her?
  • Should I have had my fellow counsellor in the same room as me when the call was in progress?

Learning Points:

• Many of the potential issues here concern the degree to which agency policy supports workers. Present agency policy at this stage, being prepared to amend it in the light of suggestions made during training.

This chapter is about what counsellors may need to do after a call in order that they and their service can survive until the phone rings again. To return to my car journey analogy for a moment, it's the equivalent of what you need to do after you've parked the car and turned off the ignition. For example, make sure you take your valuables out of the car and lock the doors. If you noticed any faults develop during your journey or a refill is required, these will have to be attended to before you take the car out again. What sort of end-of-session 'servicing' do you require before you can go back on the road again?

Whether you work for an agency or on your own, you will need to have these things in place in some form or other; don't kid yourself that you can cut corners. If your agency doesn't attend to these issues, agitate for change, provide them for yourself or don't work there. The three areas which may require attention after the call are boundaries, on-line support and record keeping.

Boundaries
The above account raises a number of issues. In terms of boundaries, many of the issues such as confidentiality/privacy hark back to those chapters covering how we might arrange things before and during the call. However, I have found that the same issues arise again the second I put the receiver down. Also, although I have separated 'boundaries' from 'on-line support', 'debriefing' and 'record keeping', there is overlap between all three as I will try to demonstrate.

When I put the telephone down on a counselling session, I often experience a deep desire to talk about the call. This desire is frequently complemented by an equally strong desire on the part of other counsellors on duty to be told about the call. However we might try to dress these urges up as some kind of professional development or 'spot supervision', the probable truth to be faced is that we like to have a good natter about the work that we do. We would do well to ask ourselves some questions about these needs and how we can go about getting them met whilst staying true to our professional principles of respect for those we are trying to help:

- *Why* do I have the need to talk about clients?
- *What* aspects of an individual call is it most helpful to talk about?
- *What* feelings do I have about this caller and his/her life?
- *How* should I talk about another person's personal life?
- *Where* is it best to talk about the content of individual calls and my reaction to them?
- *When* is it best to talk about my thoughts and feelings about a call or a shift?

In Training: Agencies must have some approach to supporting workers. Voluntary agencies are not exempt from this.
Method:
• The above are obvious questions to ask trainees when introducing the need for on-line support, debriefing, regular supervision or confidentiality and office routines.
• Ask trainees to brainstorm answers to the questions, collate and discuss.
Learning Points:
• Follow this with a presentation and discussion of agency policy.
• Make sure that agency policy covers all of the points mentioned. Do not breeze into training sessions on these issues without first checking that your agency policy is up to it. It is not appropriate to defend weak or non-existent agency policy.

As I pointed out in Chapter 5, privacy is different from confidentiality. In this situation we are talking about confidentiality; the need to keep the client's business within the boundary set by the call. Set against this is the occasional need for a counsellor to get support if the client's problem is particularly distressing for the counsellor concerned for whatever reason. This distress can take many forms and almost always happens when the client's problem triggers an emotional reaction in us such as anger, hurt, disgust or guilt because the problem reminds us of some sensitive issue in our own life such as unresolved grief.

Sometimes, of course, a client's problem can be just too overwhelming (that's why they've phoned a counsellor for help) and we have difficulty in listening to it without feeling overwhelmed ourselves. This sets up a tension between our need to keep a promise of confidentiality and our need for support, or the need to look after ourselves. This is where we can reasonably expect agency policy to support us.

If the agency I work for offers a confidential service (see Chapter 5) then I believe that I must honour that in between interviews. I do not want to talk about my clients in a disrespectful way in the guise of seeking support. I resolve this tension by following certain rules when getting on-line support and debriefing (see below).

Particular calls can put us under pressure to think that the boundary of the interview should be broken for other reasons. For example if we are lead to believe that the client/caller is in danger or that a third party is in danger. 'Danger' can mean almost anything here from physical or sexual abuse through to self harm or suicide. The question is *'What should I do?'* Even if I manage to get through the majority of the call without intervening, the panic really sets in when the call seems to be coming to the end :

> *'Can I really let this person go and do whatever I fear they might do?'*

And it gets even worse as soon as the receiver goes down as we worry:

> *'Did I do/say the right thing? - What if...(insert terrible outcome here)...happens; it will be all my fault. I should have persuaded them to give me their address and called the police/ambulance/Samaritans. Dash it, we ARE the Samaritans!'*

I often think it would be great if, like a basketball coach, I could shout *'TIME OUT!'* in the middle of a call and get some spot supervision.

In Training: This is a good exercise in any training session. *Method:*
• In specific role plays or practice sessions, suggest that trainees call 'time out' in the role of counsellor in front of the group and let them get spot supervision from the tutor or other members of the group.
Learning Point:
• This gives the trainees an opportunity to say 'I don't know what to do here', to share worries *and* practice giving supervision.

Unfortunately, it is not possible to do that, although there is much to be said for letting the client know that you are upset/uneasy or lost in the middle of a call (see Genuineness in Chapter 6). What I can do though is get on-line support from a colleague, backed up by supervision later.

On-line support

Anyone who has worked for any counselling agency, will know how important this kind of support is. Whether it comes from your peers or a day officer/supervisor it doesn't matter. As long as you get it *when you need it.* This means that on-line support might be asked for at two distinct times, whilst the call is in progress and immediately after it.

Some telephone agencies have technical provision for a third person (or more) to listen in to a call whilst it is in progress. This means that the person receiving the call can summon a colleague or supervisor to listen in and give support or practical help. (This technique is also used as on-line training or skill development with real calls by some agencies.) With this technology in place, it can lead to a feeling of 'never being alone' on the part of the telephone listener/counsellor. This reassurance that support is at hand can help workers tackle very difficult situations with greater confidence.

Such listening in does, however present ethical problems. Although it might feel as though the worker is never alone, the truth is that the caller now has no guarantee of privacy or confidentiality. Some agencies may only practise listening in with the permission of the caller, but it is not clear to what extent this affects the caller, call and outcome. If an agency let it be known up front in their publicity that such listening in was practised, it may put potential callers off. Some agencies do listen in without the callers permission or knowledge.

What is your agency policy on this matter, and what are your personal views about the ethics of the situation? It may help to put yourself in the position of the caller. Some agencies argue that the possible benefits outweigh the ethical problems.

There are no rules to **giving** the second kind of support; just offer your counselling skills to the person sitting next to you, and don't be afraid of physical contact when your colleagues are feeling very needy. A touch on the arm or a hug goes a long way when support is wanted. Remember that such support times have their own boundaries of confidentiality too.

When **seeking** support, I find the following rules of thumb help me to avoid the gossiping trap I referred to above:
• I want to talk about, and preferably express, my feelings rather than talk about the client, the content of their 'problem' or their feelings.
• If I must talk about the client, I want to do so respectfully. I want to talk about them and their world as I would wish my own most tender secrets talked about.
• Who or what in my life does the client and their world remind me of?
• What do I need to do, or talk about, right now so that I can decide whether to take another call or withdraw from duty for the rest of the session?
• What issues do I want to take to supervision as a result of this call?

If I can stick to these rules I stand a reasonable chance of meeting my immediate and urgent need for support and making the most of a potentially wonderful learning situation. Of course it goes without saying that in the heat of the moment when I most need my helpful rules, I am least likely to remember them. If these rules seem to make sense to you, or you have some good ones of your own, share them with your colleagues and incorporate them into your training. In this way the colleagues to whom you go for support can act as your memory for you. You might even consider sticking the rules up on the office wall.

Debriefing
Earlier in this book I introduced the notion of briefing before a shift or duty. The term debriefing has two meanings. Firstly it is used to mean an end-of-shift wash-up session where any issues that arose

during the shift can be identified, logged and passed on to the next shift if appropriate. Duty supervisors can close down any unresolved issues or refer them on to future training or supervision sessions. Workers feeling a bit ragged can let off steam, wind down or ask for spot supervision or support before they go home. This type of debriefing need not be lengthy, but it does go a long way to ensuring that everyone is in a fit state to make the journey home safely and that they won't be too much of a burden to their friends or family when the get there.

The second meaning of the term debriefing is as a particular activity which happens after critical incidents. Critical incident debriefing is the support offered to witnesses and emergency services after a disaster or accident at work. In terms of telephone helping and counselling work, this might mean a set support procedure which happens every time a worker receives a very distressing or abusive call. It gives the worker an opportunity to recover from the shock of the event, discharge some of the pent-up feelings associated with the event, review what actually happened and if necessary make a statement or file a report.

I suggest the following areas are covered in a debriefing session after a distressing call:

Focus on feelings
• What feelings are still around now?
• What did, or do you, want to do - to, for, or with the caller? (Cure, punish, heal, protect, take home and look after, run away from, hit, etc.)

Focus on facts
• What actually happened?
• Was any action taken?
• Is any action necessary?

Focus on learning and support
• What can be learned from this call?
• What supervision issues are raised?
• What support is necessary before you go?

After a distressing call or upsetting shift, do make sure that workers are adequately taken care of. This means many things from giving them an opportunity to let off steam, take a breather during the shift, get debriefing, through to making sure they don't drive or walk home alone.

Record keeping

I suppose there are many candidates for the 'Good-idea-in-theory-but-not-done-in-practice' award when it comes to agency policy and one of the strongest contenders would be record keeping. We all say we will do it, we all tell our colleagues we do it, we all kid ourselves that we really *do* do it. But we don't, at least not as frequently and as completely as we should. There are a number of good reasons why keeping records is a good idea:

1. **As a memory aid.** When you get any sort of decent case load, you'll find that your memory soon becomes exhausted. You can refresh yourself before a client is due in a face-to-face interview or quickly get a client's file out when they phone up for a counselling session. Always have the record file within reach of the phone or the phone on a long lead!

2. **Personal and professional development.** Good records can be a boon in supervision and will prove indispensable if you apply for BAC accreditation as a counsellor. Also, when you get long in the tooth and want to publish your grand theory of counselling, you will want to refer back through your case records to pull together the evidence. I really wish I'd kept mine!

3. **Lies, damned lies and statistics.** If you ever need to justify your existence as a counsellor you will suddenly appreciate the need for evidence of effectiveness and efficiency. The basis for much of what managers feel is acceptable evidence are accurate records. In the 1990s this holds true as much for voluntary organisations fighting for funding as it does for local government services.

4. **Monitoring.** Similar to number 3, monitoring is for example checking your clients (and staff) to see that you are fulfilling your promises to be an equal opportunities service or that you really are meeting the needs of your target client group.

5. It is agency policy. Ah yes, well, there's no getting away from this one. If you agreed to keep records you can't really carp about it now.

6. Protection. If a client complains that they have been damaged in some way by your service, it will help to have accurate records of your relationship with dates and times etc.

These good reasons for keeping records raise some ethical, personal, and possibly legal, issues.

As far as the **legal issues** are concerned, these are relatively straightforward. Firstly, before you put any information on a computer which may include the names and addresses or telephone numbers of clients or staff, check if you need to register under the Data Protection Act. Secondly, refer to *'Counselling Confidentiality and the Law'* by Tim Bond (see appendix, p.195) for an account of the legal position on confidentiality and security of information. Other people, including the police, have few legal rights to any information you hold even when a serious criminal offence may be involved. Finally on the legal side, you have to consider your client's rights to seek damages from you if you have promised to keep their records confidential and fail to do so. For example, if your office was burgled and your files were to get into the wrong hands, details of your client's lives and identities could leak out causing distress.

Ethical and personal issues are more complicated since we each bring our own personal values and ethics to the situation along with those we adhere to as responsible counsellors. I have chosen the following to illustrate some general issues. You may well have special concerns of your own.

Some counsellors feel that record keeping is not in accord with their personal qualities and say something like, *'I am a caring counsellor and will remember every single detail of all of my client's lives forever.'* Others may feel that record keeping in some way contaminates their theoretical position and skill base and say something like *'Keeping records will encourage me to think in general terms and categorise my clients. When I next speak to them, I might only remember the false categorisations, not the real person.'*

I offer the following suggestions regarding record keeping which may help overcome these and other reservations you may have. The key to secure records is to never keep all of the information relating to one client in the same physical place. When I say 'physical place' I mean different filing cabinets, different rooms or different parts of a computer programme which can never be combined on the screen or which require different passwords to gain access.

I prefer to split the information up into three pieces each recorded on cards in a card file as follows:

```
Card 1:

Name                    Client number
Address
Telephone number home
Telephone number 2
Telephone number 3
Telephone number 4
```

Keep these cards in alphabetical order - they are your **Contact Cards** and would be used if you want to contact a client for any reason whatsoever or more usually if you want to locate their other files. You may be wondering why there are four telephone number options. Some agencies will phone a client back to save the client the expense and hassle of putting coins into a call box. (Nothing is worse that trying to talk about your problems when you are more concerned about your money running out.) If your client is a regular caller, s/he may have favourite locations from which they call, you can make a note of these on the card rather than writing the numbers down each time they call.

Card 2:

Name   Client Number
Brief Address:
Demographic details: e.g. Age, sex, ethnic origin,
disabled employment status, etc. for monitoring
purposes.
Referred from: e.g. Self, other agency, etc.
Referred to:
Presenting problem:
Coded list of problem types, e.g.
        1=financial
        2=accommodation incl. homelessness
        3=personal/sexual
        4=personal/educational, etc.
First session date:
Counsellor: (some agencies have numbers or codes)
Final session date:
Counsellor:
Return date: (if client re-presents, start another card
and enter card number here)
Counsellor:

These are your **Statistics and Monitoring Cards** and should be kept
in client number order. The list on the card is not meant to be
exhaustive, but it gives you an idea of the kind of information it may
be useful or necessary to collect. You will be able to discover how
many women and men used your service, what the age profile of
your clientele is, whether your service is used by different ethnic
groups, who refers the most clients to you, which areas of town they
come from etc. This information will be invaluable in
        i) your annual report to justify your funding, and
        ii) your analysis of the effectiveness of your service.
It's always more interesting to see who doesn't use your service,

rather than who does. This will tell you whether you are really open access (if that is your aim). You may need to find out why four times as many women aged fifteen to twenty phone up than any other age group.

Card 3

Call record   Client number

Dates:
Times:
Duration:

Issues discussed:
Action taken:
Counsellor:

These cards are the **Case Note Cards** and should also be kept in client number order. Note that the clients can't be identified from this card alone, and although they can be identified from the other cards, no-one can tell why they have contacted your service, since the presenting problem section should be in your code. These cards are useful for case discussions and reviews, group supervision, agency planning, and statistical reporting since you will be able to show how many client sessions the agency provided, how many each client had on average etc.

There's one final type of record that I like to keep and that's my own personal log or counselling journal. I keep my personal record of each client contact session both on the phone and face-to-face. Clients can be referred to by any code you choose. I allocate one sheet to each session and divide the page up into three sections:
    1. What the client talked about.
    2. How I felt today - how I felt towards the client, was the session very tiring, was I bored, excited, distracted etc.

3. How I thought I performed in the session today; what supervision issues were raised.

I know that a number of counsellors keep similar personal journals and I can highly recommend it as a good method of getting the very best out of your supervision sessions and turning every session with a client into a potentially wonderful learning experience. It also helps avoid the problem of letting my thinking become too rigid and compartmentalised through all this record keeping. The process becomes much more personal, fluid and creative and makes a great contribution to my personal and professional development.

9 Between Calls

This chapter is concerned with the between-journey maintenance all cars need to stay on the road. What do we as counsellors need to do between duties or clients to maintain ourselves, to prevent burn-out and to further develop ourselves so that we continually improve? These activities are differentiated from those mentioned in the last chapter by virtue of the fact that these are not related to the last call you received. These activities are to do with your whole process of being a telephone helper/counsellor.

Such activities are referred to in the counselling world as, for example, on-going professional development (e.g. training), ongoing personal maintenance and development (e.g. personal therapy) or burn-out avoidance, etc. Professional bodies such as the BAC require counsellors to provide evidence that these areas of self-maintenance and development are being actively pursued. For some counsellors, a single space which has the potential to achieve all of this and a good deal more is called *supervision*. However, I will outline the range of self-maintenance and development activities and briefly look at them all whilst concentrating on the primary activity of supervision.

The idea of maintaining and developing our personal and professional selves is not new. Supervision and support have been written about in many places throughout this book and, as I have also pointed out, supervision is now universally recognised as an essential component of a counsellor's professional activities. By 'professional' I do not mean that you have to be paid for your counselling, rather that if you consider yourself to be a counsellor or using counselling skills substantially, then your work should be of a professional standard. You will also notice that I have been at pains to point out that the activities in question not only maintain our selves but also have a developmental function. We should not be satisfied with just keeping our skills, attitudes and competencies in trim, we should be actively trying to increase our range and depth.

Self maintenance and development can be initially sub-divided into personal and professional categories:

Personal

Personal therapy.

• Attending self-development events related to counselling, e.g. encounter groups.

• Taking reasonable breaks from telephone work.

• Hobbies and pastimes.

• Supervision.

Professional

• Continuing training (e.g. short courses or further longer qualification-oriented training).

• Attending appropriate agency-specific or counselling-related conferences.

• Applying for BAC Accreditation as a counsellor.

• Taking on new, challenging work.

• Supervision.

This list is not intended to be exhaustive. It is there to help you think of the range of activities that telephone counsellors could consider to be making a contribution to their personal and professional development and maintenance. Training, attending conferences, personal therapy and supervision are the obvious activities, with ongoing training and supervision being the responsibility of the agency. It is reasonable to expect the employers of telephone helper/counsellors to provide or pay for ongoing training and supervision, or if you are a volunteer, that the agency provide these free of charge for you. Training is covered in part in several places throughout this book, now it is time to pay closer attention to supervision.

What is supervision?

Many people engaged in helping have found their own ways of getting support. Maybe through talking to friends, colleagues, family etc. Such informal arrangements have drawbacks, firstly they are OK for emergencies but lack any real potential for learning and development and secondly confidentiality is always a problem. The third disadvantage is that however devoted to you and your work they are, your family and friends may soon get sick of it. Finally, there is no way that these informal arrangements can ensure ethical practice, since there are no real sanctions that your friends and colleagues can impose upon your practice.

The word 'supervision' is another word which whilst becoming more common in general helping settings, it is still prone to misinterpretation. Some suggest it would help if we said 'counsellor supervision' instead, but I think that this may limit a brilliant idea to the select few. Supervision used in the counselling context does not mean line management; does not imply control, permission or discipline; is not linked with authority or direction and has little to do with the idea of overseeing probation or trial periods. It is not limited to casework supervision, nor does it map completely on to the emerging practice of clinical supervision in nursing.

In contrast to these other activities, counsellor supervision has the following elements:
   •Facilitation of personal and professional development.
   •Personal and professional support and challenge.
   •Promotion and development of counselling skills.
   •Maintenance and development of ethical practice.
   •Promotion of accountable counselling practice and services.
   •Congruence with counselling values.

Brigid Proctor and Francesca Inskipp have developed a functional map of supervision which suggests that counselling supervision has three elements:
   • Formative: Developing professional skills and attitudes, and personal qualities.
   • Normative:Monitoring ethical practice within professional guidelines.
   • Restorative: Repairing and restoring depleted personal resources.
They argue that good supervision provides these three functions and there is no reason to suggest that telephone counselling requires supervision any less frequently or with any different emphases. Indeed, if telephone counselling is all the more difficult because of the differences of the communications medium, then we might argue that telephone workers require more supervision than face-to-face

counsellors. Proctor and Inskipp have written extensively on supervision, including training packs covering how practitioners can make the most of being a supervisee (Proctor and Inskipp 1993) and how to develop the necessary skills to become an effective supervisor (Proctor and Inskipp 1995) see Appendix p.195.

Telephone counsellors should take great care when choosing a supervisor. It is essential to have access to either a supervisor or consultant who has reasonable experience of working on the telephone. It is a mistake to believe that skilled face-to-face supervisors can transfer sufficient knowledge and skills to the telephone situation. Your supervisor will also need to be briefed on agency policy and procedures.

In addition to choosing your supervisor on the basis of their telephone background, it is just as important to look at their theoretical approach to counselling. You may decide that this point in the development of your telephone counselling practice requires you to have a supervisor from the same theoretical background as yourself. On the other hand some counsellors believe that they have more to gain from working with a supervisor who might challenge some of the assumptions they make when working with clients. In my case, as a Person-Centred counsellor I have currently chosen a supervisor who shares my theoretical orientation. I expect my supervisor to provide the core conditions in supervision. These are the conditions which I believe are necessary before any beneficial support, learning or development can take place. I expect to meet my supervisor as an equal but with different roles in the relationship.

Many people worry about the boundaries of supervision, i.e. what is acceptable and valid as a supervision issue and what is not. My own view is that anything and everything that arises in my life which may affect my work with clients is admissible. So for me, that includes just about everything from discovering that the reason I am getting nowhere with my client is because her voice reminds me of my ex-wife, to being depressed because I'm fed up at work, and even including whether Aston Villa won on Saturday. Like counselling itself, the boundaries in supervision are best managed by a contract between the supervisor and supervisee.

Who, where, how and for how long?

This book is not about supervision, but I do know that very few agencies or individuals providing a telephone service pay enough attention to supervision. They fall short of good practice because they believe they haven't got the resources to provide adequate supervision. Whilst I (as a supervisor and supervisee) know that supervision, like counselling, is a skill that takes time to acquire, I also know that many voluntary organisations must do the very best they can with what they've got. Professional bodies are making ever stronger statements about the need for appropriate and sufficient supervision. The BAC state unequivocally in their Code of Ethics and Practice for Counsellors that:

> 'It is a breach of the ethical requirement for counsellors to practice without regular counselling supervision/consultative support.' (para B3.1)
>
> The Volume of supervision should be in proportion to the volume of counselling work undertaken and the experience of the counsellor.' (para B3.4)

BAC also make recommendations for the amount of supervision for face-to-face counselling work. As yet, there are no published guidelines for telephone counselling work, but it is reasonable to assume that telephone counselling will require at least the same levels of supervision as face-to-face work, possibly higher.

General guidelines for supervision of telephone counsellors:

> (Note that the calculation of the number of hours supervision for telephone work needs to take into account the type and length of the calls. For example, shorter, less demanding calls may require less frequent and/or different supervision than longer, more intense, demanding calls. To assess the right rate and type of supervision for your work, it might be necessary to ask an independent consultant or supervisor to advise in consultation with agency staff.)

• Supervision, whether individual or group, should not be less frequent than once per month otherwise the lack of continuity will be too disruptive to the development of a good supervisory relationship.

• 0 - 5 substantial client calls per week requires around 1 hour supervision per month.
• 5 - 10 substantial client calls per week requires around 1 hour supervision per fortnight.
• 10 - 20 substantial client calls per week requires around 1 hour supervision per week.
• Several supervisees together with one supervisor at the same time is called group supervision. It doesn't save any time at all, since each supervisee should be allocated the same time pro-rata as in individual supervision. There are other benefits in terms of learning from each other's experiences and the sense of support and togetherness we get from working in a team.
• Get hold of current copies of the following BAC Codes of Ethics and Practice (see Appendix p.193):
    i)   for Counselling Skills,
    ii) for Counsellors,
    iii for Supervisors,
    iv) for Trainers.

Organising support and supervision for telephone work
Making the commitment to appropriate on-going support and supervision is the first step. Next comes organising this for yourself, or for others in an agency. The type of support and supervision required will, of course, depend upon the nature of the helping activity being undertaken. It is important to identify quite what level of counselling-related help is being offered. Chapter 2 might be a good starting point, followed by looking at the BAC Code of Ethics and Practice for Counselling Skills.

If telephone counselling is the activity, then *supervision* is required. If counselling skills are being used to supplement advice, information or a listening service, then some other kind of support may suffice, but there is every reason to suppose that supervision would still be appropriate. The important message is that support for telephone helper/counsellors is not something that should be under-resourced. The guidelines are there because BAC and others have undertaken lengthy consultative processes with a wide range of professionals and these guidelines continue to be refined by the democratic process within the bodies concerned. They currently represent best practice and we would dismiss them at our peril.

My constant references to good practice have implications beyond simply trying to follow the appropriate codes and guidelines. Supervision is supposed to be a challenging activity as well as a supportive one. If it is not organised well it can simply become a rather limp self-congratulatory exercise in which we talk about how much we have helped out clients without ever seriously questioning our effectiveness as helpers. This can happen at agency level too. For these reasons it is good practice, if not essential, that the supervision be independent or external to the helper/counsellor and agency. By independent, I mean that the supervisor is not in any dual relationships with either the individual helper/counsellor or the agency. A dual relationship is where the supervisor might be a line manager, friend or colleague of the individual or an employee, trainer or consultant in another capacity with the agency. Such dual relationships might compromise the integrity of any recommendations that a supervisor may make.

A supervisor may well make recommendations regarding professional and ethical best practice in a specific client case, work load of the telephone worker, competence and suitability of the worker for the work in question, agency policy, etc. The individual telephone helper/counsellor and/or the agency must be prepared to look at and respond constructively (rather than defensively) to the issues raised by the supervisor. Sometimes this may have policy implications, financial and funding implications, selection and recruitment implications, training implications, or implications for the continued employment of certain helpers/counsellors.

The next section describes some popular ways of organising the supervision and support of telephone helping/counselling. There may be other ways of organising this important area of activity whilst remembering that best practice would suggest supervision that is *formative, normative and restorative,* is conducted by appropriately qualified people and at an appropriate frequency according to workload.

Supervision

This is where one person is identified as the supervisor and may be more experienced that the supervisee. They meet on a one-to-one basis at a frequency determined by the rate at which the supervisee is working with client calls (see above). The supervisor would usually be a fully qualified counsellor (Diploma level) with substantial telephone experience. You might further require them to have experience of the work area in which you are involved, e.g. Gay Switchboard, employee assistance work, etc. It would also be good practice to expect a supervisor to have undergone supervision training (see appendix p.195). Finally the supervisor would not be in a dual relationship with the agency or individual, see above.

Group supervision

When more than one supervisee meets with someone identified as a supervisor, it is called group supervision. The skills required of the supervisee are much the same as in individual supervision, but there are different advantages for the supervisees. Group supervision provides more material for supervisees to develop by learning from the experiences of others. Set against this is the disincentive to raise sensitive issues or work on practice that is less than perfect in a more public setting.

Group supervision should be led by an experienced supervisor or by negotiating a shared supervisory role if the counsellors are fully qualified and experienced (called *peer group supervision*). Peer group supervision is not suitable for inexperienced counsellors.

Co-supervision

Co-supervision is seen as a popular solution when the money is short. What happens is this: two counsellors agree to pair up in a co-supervision relationship. Each supervision meeting lasts say two hours, each taking one hour as supervisee, whilst acting as supervisor to the other for the remaining hour. Co-supervision can work very well with experienced helper/counsellors, but with newly qualified persons it might lack some essential qualities in terms of being formative and normative (see p.159).

Support group

I have made a distinction here between support and supervision groups, because I really do think that running a supervision group is too skilled a task for inexperienced helper/counsellors. The differences are that a support group need not have an identified leader. This boundary-keeping role can either be shared or can rotate around group members from meeting to meeting. Working in a group has several benefits. Development of social skills, learning through exposure to a wide range of views and experiences, seeing many different ways of solving problems and that sense of *belonging* are all available only through working in groups.

A leaderless support group could orient itself towards supervision issues by having regular meetings which were carefully boundaried. No gossiping, socialising or tea-making. Participants could take responsibility for bringing 'supervision' issues and being supported by the group whilst they explored the issue they had brought.

Support network

An extension of the supervision group whereby after exchanging telephone numbers and addresses we agree to give 'spot support' if something arises out of our work with clients between support group meetings. This can happen face-to-face or over the telephone. Such support networks will need to evolve some groundrules regarding access, etc. (i.e. do we offer the support anytime, on demand or by arrangement?) There will also need to be rules regarding gossiping and using the network for social relationships.

Special training events

One of the things that happened to me after I finished my counsellor training was that I felt a great thirst for more training. It was a combination of i) feeling lost without the chums I had spent a year going through thick and thin with, and ii) thinking that I had only just chipped the surface of counselling skills and that there was so much to learn!

Occasional 'touchdowns' to training are a good idea since no training is a complete preparation for telephone helping. Intermittent special events for telephone helper/counsellors in an agency help them express their commitment to on-going professional development and help the agency update their workers on new developments, specialist areas, changes in agency policy, team building, or whatever. A programme of meetings advertised well in advance is the best way of doing it, perhaps occasionally inviting guest speakers or trainers if funds allow.

On-going professional development is something to which all helper/counsellor members of BAC are committed. One of the easiest ways of achieving this is through a programme of on-going training. In all this talk of on-going training, having appropriate basic qualifications must not be ignored. One of the most stressing events for individual telephone helper/counsellors is the feeling that they are out of their depth and might be damaging the caller. If you are doing genuine counselling work on the telephone you will need more than a counselling skills qualification.

The ideal solution?
Support and supervision eat up the precious resources of money, time and effort in all organisations, voluntary or otherwise. Agency workers are always trying to make effectiveness and efficiency meet happily to provide the best service for clients. A good plan for delivering supervision and support on a budget is to arrange co-supervision in addition to a support group running in parallel. The support group could then join up with others in your agency for the occasional special training event. If your agency does not have a system of support and supervision, there's nothing to stop you from organising one yourself. The minimum you need is a willing partner and you're off. Add four more and you've got a support group.

Training as a supervisee and supervisor
Inskipp and Proctor (1993) have alerted the counselling world to the waste of time and resources spent in the first few supervision sessions as the supervisee grapples with the task (and still sometimes doesn't seem to grasp the purpose). Whilst we could say that this is all part of the developmental process and that in the hands of a competent supervisor all will be well, the fact is that callers may be

receiving a degraded service whilst the counsellor learns how to use supervision 'properly'. This learning doesn't have to happen by chance or 'natural development'. It can be deliberately planned for and an increasing number of training courses are including 'supervisee skills' as part of the training. For those agencies and individuals who haven't got the staff expertise and resources to deliver such training, a workbook plus audio-tapes by Inskipp and Proctor (1993) is available, see Appendix, p.195.

There is a small and increasing number of supervision training courses and as I mentioned above, depending upon the location, it might be difficult or impossible to find a trained supervisor with the experience appropriate for your needs. Agencies may well decide to invest in training their own supervisors, either to supplement independent consultative supervision, or to develop an in-house supervision network. I should say at this stage, that every agency must have some sort of external, independent consultant supervisor for the reasons outlined earlier in this chapter.

Growing your own supervisors is also made easier for agencies by further training resources developed by Inskipp and Proctor (1995) which could also be used by individual helper/counsellors wishing to develop support and supervision skills. The comprehensive programme comprises a workbook and audio tapes. This and other supervision publications are listed in the Appendix, p.195.

Hints for first-time supervisors
If you are setting up a co-supervision relationship or support group for the first time and you've never been a supervisor or experienced supervision as a supervisee before, here are some simple guidelines to help you:
- Don't be afraid. If your intention is to create a safe environment in which you can help your partner learn from their experience, you won't go far wrong.
- Set off with the further intention of offering the core conditions to your partner.
- Listen carefully to what they are saying; seek clarification if you're not understanding fully.

- Help them explore their concerns using role-plays, looking at notes, talking to imaginary clients or whatever method seems appropriate.
- Can you see any links or connections between the issues and concerns that s/he brings.
- Look for patterns of feelings, thoughts and behaviours in what your partner is saying and in their work with their clients.
- Ask your partner if what s/he is saying sounds familiar to them or has echoes in other areas of their lives.
- Challenge your partner to look deeply into their experience. Don't be afraid to question what they are saying.

These guidelines work just as well in a support group, where you may decide that the role of 'facilitator' is to rotate from meeting to meeting or be shared by all group members.

Whatever you decide to do, good luck and remember that your basic tool-kit is you and the core conditions. After proper training, you will never be without it. Do not sell yourself short on support and supervision, your life may depend upon it. We are all now familiar with the term 'burn-out' and it has been suggested that one of the main causes of burn-out is insufficient opportunities for supervision, support and continuing training. Ways of avoiding it include:

- Making arrangements for support and supervision (and keeping to them!).
- Attending training workshops and taking further qualifications.
- Looking after your physical health.
- Taking appropriate breaks.
- Keeping to a reasonable work schedule; do not work shifts that are too long, take a break after a difficult call.
- Bringing variety into your counselling work and life in general.
- Agencies and organisations must support individual telephone counsellor/helpers in this; do not work for an agency which exploits workers at the expense of the worker and, eventually, the caller. It is unethical.
- All of these remedies can be monitored through supervision.

10 Research into Telephone Helping and Counselling

Before launching into a summary of research findings on the subject of telephone helping and counselling I think it is important to realise that there has been very little published on the subject of telephone helping and counselling. Add to that the notion that what has been published may go out of date quite quickly because it often comments upon elements of helpline organisation, practice or volunteer training which have been superseded by better practice as standards generally improve. In addition, there is the effect of changes in technology and the meaning of communications technology to an increasingly technologically-literate group of service users. The final caution is that none of the research that adopts a scientific model is so far replicated and thus cannot be said to 'prove' anything. The most that can be said is that some of the following research might 'suggest' some courses of action.

I have grouped the papers into topics and provide a very brief summary of each paper in terms of the methods used and the major findings. This is not intended to be a comprehensive literature review, but should provide some food for thought. Although some of the titles might contain jargon which some readers will find confusing, I have tried to give as jargon-free a summary as possible. Don't think that you will not understand the summary if you can't understand the title. The research reviewed is not included because it is methodologically sound, it is here in order to provoke thought.

If you wish to search the literature for further research, perhaps on a given theme connected with telephone counselling, you may be able to gain reference access to your local university library for a small fee. If you have a computer linked to the Internet or E-mail you also may be able to access other library facilities or bulletin boards.

Readers will also note that the research reviewed here is not up-to-the-minute or state-of-the-art. This is deliberate in one sense since I do not want to give the impression that telephone helping is research driven. It is not, and stands little chance of being overly influenced by research in the foreseeable future. There are some good reasons for this. Firstly, the majority of telephone helping agencies are locally configured to answer a local need. Service development should be informed by local research rather than international trends. Secondly, there is just not enough research in this area to demonstrate anything conclusive, (see above). Thirdly, some research dates very quickly. I have chosen research which is trying to make very general points that are still current.

What follows is included for much more than curiosity value, however. Since all telephone helping service organisers should be committed to continuously evaluating their service in terms of effectiveness. Some of this research has some good suggestions regarding methods of evaluation. Readers should find it all thought-provoking and who knows, some may be inspired to do some research of their own in an area that is badly under-represented in the literature.

General evaluation of services and calls
I have separated some papers on suicide prevention into their own topic area, so the articles in the current section are of a more general nature. [Any comments I make are in square brackets.]

1. *Crisis Telephone Counselors' Views of Clinical Interaction Situations.* Steven Walfish, Community Mental Health Journal, Vol.19, No.3. 1983.
   Method:
   Walfish constructed a questionnaire which he called the Telephone Counseling Clinical Interaction Inventory and sent it out to all 105 volunteer crisis telephone counsellors at Life Crisis

Services in St Louis, Missouri. The volunteers were asked to rate situations on a scale from 'Extremely Uncomfortable' to 'Extremely Comfortable'.

Some examples of the statements are:
- The client says, 'I want to hurt myself.'
- The client says 'I've just taken a bottle of pills.'
- The client is masturbating.
- The client says 'Go fuck yourself'.'
- A male client says, 'I've just had sex with my daughter.'

The idea was to find out which situations were most frequently encountered and which the volunteers either had most difficulty in dealing with or felt most uncomfortable during.

Findings

32 of the 100 statements issued to the volunteers showed high levels of counsellor discomfort. Walfish examined the responses in detail and subjected them to statistical analysis which indicated that:
- Unsurprisingly, women volunteers were more uncomfortable than male volunteers when a male caller talks in explicit sexual terms.
- Men felt less comfortable than women when the caller asks 'What's your name?'
- Younger volunteers felt more uncomfortable than older volunteers when the caller asks, 'Do you love me?'
- The majority of volunteers had difficulty with suicidal clients. Walfish speculates that this might be due to the counsellor's inappropriate sense of responsibility.
- Obscene callers also caused great discomfort to all counsellors, (but particularly women as the object of such calls).
- Counsellors had difficulty when callers expressed negative (e.g. anger) or positive feelings towards them.
- Counsellors became frustrated when clients refused to engage in a 'meaningful' interaction with them.
- Finally counsellors had very real discomfort and difficulty in dealing with problems of physical and sexual abuse.

Walfish discusses the possibility that the difficulties arise from skill deficits (since the volunteers were not trained professional counsellors) and suggests that telephone counsellors should be better trained to deal with genuine 'clinical' situations on the telephone.

2. Does Telephone Counselling Have Preventive Value?
Andrew R. Hornblow, Australian and New Zealand Journal of Psychiatry, Vol. 20, pp23-28, 1986.

Method

This is a review of research in which Hornblow surveys some 60 or so papers [hardly any UK work], looking at their findings in terms of primary, secondary and tertiary prevention. These he defines as:

Primary: attempting to 'reduce the incidence of disorder'.

Secondary: 'identify and treat as soon as possible so as to reduce the length and severity of the disorder'.

Tertiary: reduce the level of handicap or impairment from a disorder that already exists.

[Readers may not find this categorisation very helpful or informative.]

Findings

Although Hornblow is unable to find much direct evidence for primary prevention since most telephone service users are in crisis due to some existing complaint or life situation, Hornblow does raise an interesting point. That is, that over time, the mere existence of a telephone counselling service dedicated to a particular issue, e.g. child abuse, may raise awareness within the community to the extent that, in this case, potential perpetrators may be dissuaded from becoming active abusers and may seek help.

Hornblow finds several studies concluding that paraprofessional telephone counsellors can achieve acceptable levels of skill and empathic response with appropriate training and two studies are able to link skill level with follow-up studies of caller-satisfaction. This, along with evidence to suggest that telephone counsellors can provide effective support for identified at-risk groups, (e.g. clinical depression after death of an infant), Hornblow concludes that telephone counsellors can create the conditions necessary for effective work with callers, though attention to contracting and treatment strategies is recommended.

3. The Functioning of British Counselling Hotlines

P.K.G. Davies, British Journal of Guidance and Counselling, Vol. 10, No. 2, 1982.

Method

Davies utilised a 'mystery caller' method in which a role-player called 10 counselling hotlines in the West Midlands and presented them with a personal problem. The call was started in each case by the caller asking whether the agency could help with personal problems and the male caller revealed his problem to be that his family wished him to get married. The caller then let the conversation be led (or otherwise) by the helpline counsellor. The role-player rated the counsellors' responses using a five-point scale similar to the ones designed by Carkhuff (1969) for assessing accurate empathy, positive regard and genuineness. Some effort was made to adjust the ratings according to the length of the call. Each call was analysed briefly with example transcripts. This 'cold-calling' method may raise ethical issues.

Findings

The example responses quoted by Davies range from the horrendous to reasonably skilful. His findings in general are not flattering to the services in the study and he concludes that agencies need a higher standard of basic training, particularly simple listening and reflective skills. He further suggests that agencies tend to over-promote their services and should attend to more responsible, accurate publicity, along with periodic evaluations of effectiveness using 'mystery callers'.

4. Relateline: an Evaluation of a Telephone Helpline Counselling Service for Marital Problems

Patricia A. Hunt, British Journal of Guidance and Counselling, Vol.21, No.3, 1993.

Method

Cheshire Relate started a telephone helpline in order to manage an ever growing waiting list for their face-to-face service. Careful record keeping allowed this study to evaluate the service using one year's calls. The method involved gathering information from record and log books, computing and presenting statistical information, analysing most frequently presented problems, evaluating the value of the service and finally interviewing a sample of Helpline workers using a short six-question structured interview.

Findings

Too many general findings to summarise here, ranging from information about call type and frequency, demographic details of callers, through to costs of service. The paper includes discussion of repeat callers [termed follow-up calls by Hunt], gender of callers, hoax calls and the counsellors responses.

Hunt concludes that the Helpline provides a valuable service for Relate clients, whilst noting the high cost of the service [Relate is nowadays more concerned about funding]. On the subject of training, she notes that telephone counselling is different to face-to-face counselling (and probably more difficult). It requires extra training in specific telephone skills and issues. Finally Hunt predicts a growth in telephone work and offers a critical opinion on the 'start a helpline' knee-jerk reaction to every new crisis or problem.

[All in all, a great example of evaluation in practice and the benefits of keeping good, comprehensive records. All helpline managers should read this paper to see how evaluation of the service can help monitor and improve the service.]

Suicidal callers

5. *Strategies for Suicide Intervention by Telephone*
Jennifer Hinson, Suicide and Life Threatening Behaviour, Vol.2, No.3, 1982.

Method

Not a research paper, this article suggests strategies for preventing the suicidal caller from making an attempt upon their own life. If this is your aim, then this paper proposes a model in which, the counsellor will try, 'any feasible intervention technique....anything short of playing God,' in order stop the suicidal caller. The model proposed is integrative with strong cognitive/reality flavours, is affirmative and life-oriented, and is based on the idea that the suicidal person is unable to make sensible decisions due to diminished judgement.

Findings

A crude summary of the model is:
• Never underestimate the caller's intentions.
• The relationship should be seen as parent-child, with the counsellor as the authoritative parent.
• Don't use euphemisms, be direct and use reality therapy, i.e. say 'killing yourself' not 'suicide'.
• Counsellor should communicate confidence and competence.
• Do not over question caller.
• Challenge irrational beliefs.
• Get the caller to think more about the issues.
• Combat hopelessness by making positive suggestions.
• Demonstrate understanding by active listening.
• Leave the caller feeling good that they have called.
• Extract two promises; one, that he won't kill himself and two, that he follows a contract to look at alternatives to killing himself.

[This model is an extreme version of many that aim to prevent suicide or provide a 'holding' intervention in a crisis. This type of model may well be too interventionist for many agencies and individuals.]

6. Therapeutic Management of Chronic Callers to a Suicide Prevention Centre
Barry C. Barman, Journal of Community Psychology, Vol.8, pp45-48, 1980.

Method

Barman compared two groups of chronic callers each receiving different treatment strategies at the Suicide Prevention and Crisis service of Columbus, Ohio. One group received the usual volunteer responses (setting up a predetermined time limit for the call and keeping a list of chronic callers with a specific plan for working with each caller) whilst the 'treatment' group received a new treatment strategy designed to a) reduce the frequency of their calls and b) persuade callers to become more specific when discussing their problem.

The treatment strategy consisted of *active telephone counselling* where one counsellor is assigned to each chronic caller and made a contract with the chronic caller to make regular weekly calls (the counsellor would call the client) at an appointed time. The weekly call-rate was reduced gradually over a period of time. The number of calls made by the chronic callers were monitored during the seven-week treatment programme and during a 9-week follow-up period.

Findings

The number of calls made by the control group did not vary. The number of calls made by the treatment group was significantly reduced over the treatment period and this reduction was maintained for the nine-week follow-up period. Barman concludes that actively managing the treatment of chronic callers is effective, suggesting that genuine telephone counselling is not only possible but also effective.

7. *Chronic Callers to a Suicide Prevention Center*
David Lester and Gene W. Brockopp, Community Mental Health Journal, Vol.6. No.3, 1970

Method

The characteristics of 24 chronic callers (having called the centre at least 10 times) to a suicide prevention centre at Erie County (USA) were reviewed and categorised. Lester and Brockopp noted that only 20% of the callers to the suicide prevention centre were actually suicidal. Some were 'chronic callers' and one caller had called the centre 173 times in 8 months.

Findings

Lester and Brockopp extracted the following 4 categories of chronic caller from their data:

• Seven callers were seeing other therapists and used the center to criticise their therapist, relieve anxieties about therapy or generally supplement therapy.

• Two callers were seeking specific treatment and used the centre to help them.

• Six callers with no history of psychiatric illness called the centre regularly to 'ventilate their feelings.'

• Nine callers who had previously received psychiatric treatment and appeared to be currently disturbed called to 'ventilate their feelings and pursue their delusions.'

Lester and Brockopp noted that of the 24 callers, 11 gave no indication of being suicidal (either in the past or the present) and concluded that the chronic callers were probably no more suicidal than other callers, but because of the repeated calls they gave the centre a better chance of making a positive intervention.

Four approaches to dealing with chronic callers were considered:

i) discouraging callers, ii) listening without limits, iii) limiting the time for each call and lastly, iv) identification, recording and treatment plan for each chronic caller. The authors favoured the last option, but this was not substantiated by research findings.

Training

8. *Experiences of Volunteer Telephone Counselors: A Comparison of a Professionally Oriented and a Non-professionally Oriented Approach to Their Training.*

Linda Viney, Journal of Community Psychology, Vol.11. July 1983.

Method

Viney's complicated title boils down to her looking at two groups of volunteer counsellors. The two groups represent two approaches to training; one, the professional approach, delivered as a series of lectures, emphasised knowledge, professional distance and expertise, whilst the non-professional approach involved little formal training and volunteer self-selection, emphasised peer-helping, empathy and use of self.

The two groups came from two inner-city telephone counselling agencies staffed by volunteers in Sydney, Australia. Viney tried to match the groups for various demographic variables. She then scored the counsellors' performances after training on the basis of their own reports of their work.

Findings

Viney accompanies the findings with illustrative statements, some of which are fairly horrendous, e.g. 'This counselling kind of grows on you after a while,' and, 'I soon sorted him out.' The following differences between the groups were noted [none was statistically tested]:

In comparison to the professional group, the non-professional group:

• were more anxious regarding client behaviour,

- made more spontaneous gut-level responses,
- had an unrealistic view of their mastery of appropriate skills,
- saw themselves in a more eclectic-carer role, e.g. had little idea of boundaries,
- saw their callers as less anxious, less angry and generally in less distress,
- identified more with their callers.

Viney [in my view, understandably] has difficulty in concluding much from this study. The two groups selected do not represent typical trainings in the 1990s and are atypical of any training widely practised in the UK. The lessons may simply be a) training is important, and b) avoid lecture-based training.

11 One Voluntary Agency and Its Training

by Anna Karczewska-Slowikowska

The traditional voluntary listening helpline agency has provided the main impetus for the development of telephone helping services in the UK. Training in such agencies whilst well-intentioned can sometimes fall short of the standards required for good telephone helping. This chapter is included to give a brief first-hand account of one voluntary helpline and to share some issues arising from its training programme. The chapter's aims are to encourage readers to look at some of the issues raised elsewhere in this book and to integrate them into a coherent training experience. The context of the helpline, selection of volunteers, the role and qualities of the trainer and the organisation of training are all briefly addressed.

General issues in volunteer training

The number of telephone helplines has increased over the years and includes large organisations like the Samaritans, Childline, Parentline, smaller agencies like Family Contact Line, people working from their own homes and self help groups, media linked helplines and so forth. The creation of so many helplines can be seen as a response to a need for information and support in the community.

The emphasis of using *counselling skills* on the telephone is not therapy or personality change, but rather support and ease of accessibility in times of crisis or need. It is pragmatic; the belief is that the caller can best be helped by an individual who is caring, non-judgmental and offering a sympathetic ear, in other words, being there to *listen*.

Family Contact Line, historical perspective.
In 1974 the full facts of the tragic case of Maria Caldwell were published to a shocked and horrified public. The little child had died at the age of eight years, after systematic beatings by her stepfather. Phyllis Oldfield of Altrincham, Cheshire, wrote to her local newspaper pointing out that there was an obvious need for some kind of organisation to help families in a situation where there was a child at risk. In February 1975, this letter brought some 20 women, aged from 20 - 60 plus, together to discuss their plans. The original intention had been to set up a residential hostel for battered babies but it became apparent that this was not practical. There were agencies to care for battered babies but few to forestall attacks on children by easing the tensions which can cause these attacks. They decided to work towards opening a centre where parents could either call in or telephone if things were getting on top of them, thereby taking the steam out of a potentially explosive situation. During the spring and summer of 1975 this group of women worked at fund-raising, publicity, recruitment and training.

Just six months after the inaugural meeting, rooms over a shop in the centre of Altrincham, Cheshire were offered at an affordable rent. Posters and small handouts printed, distributed and the press, local radio and television became interested. By November 1975 a rota had been drawn up for the 55 - 60 volunteers to staff the centre and the telephone. Family Contact Line was officially opened.

Today in 1995, despite financial constraints, concerns over premises and recruitment of volunteers, the centre has increased its number of counselling rooms, staffed telephone lines and still has an ongoing supply of 50 volunteers. It has its own nursery with a fully qualified nursery co-ordinator, supervisor and volunteers. This unit operates within the requirements of social services working alongside the telephone listening service. There are members of the original committee still operating and keeping FCL in sight of the original aims and objectives. The agency arose out of a need in the community and 20 years on that need is still there and being met.

Training volunteers

My own initial voluntary training consisted of 30 hours on helpline skills. This is the bare minimum for training volunteers to acquire basic skills, there being little agreement about whether helpline volunteers need more than the most basic skills, or if having an extensive training qualification makes for a better telephone listener. However, it is my view that training only *begins* with a 10 week course and, in my experience, the majority of volunteers have access to extended, more advanced training opportunities from external specialist agencies, colleges and private trainers, up to validated counselling certificate and diploma courses. Helpline agency trainers continue to debate whether we should train for skilled technicians or well rounded practitioners. Given the limits on resources and time, my view is that the sensible approach would seem to be the training of a sensitive listener who has a repertoire of appropriate, if low-level skills.

I have organised this material on helpline agency training in the following way:
- Roles and responsibilities
- Guidelines for effective learning
- What is considered 'good training practice'
- Evaluation

Training at FCL
- Aims and objectives
- Selection and assessment of volunteers
- Trainees views of training when applied to practice - did it prepare them for the calls received?

Roles and responsibilities

My brief as trainer is to provide a basic course to prepare volunteers to handle calls. The trainer's role is to facilitate learning, and the primary method of learning is experiential, i.e. using exercises, designed to simulate calls; giving and receiving feedback; experiencing how it feels to be a person in distress, etc. Attention needs to be given to fears that they will have to expose themselves, to experiences they would rather not have, feeling humiliated in public, feeling pressured into doing things or saying things they do not wish to. These fears need to be attended to in the training programme, and both content and methods should be explained to trainees from the outset. Volunteers have enormous personal potential and great resources as a result of their own life experiences. In my training role, my task is to help them draw on and make best use of these resources.

In voluntary settings, the role of trainer is taken on by someone with little or no formal training or teaching experience or qualifications. General helpline experience, sensitivity, and an interest in training, are taken as sufficient qualifications for this work. The British Association for Counselling has recently introduced a pilot scheme for the Accreditation of Counsellor Trainers and Counselling Skills Trainer, laying down minimum levels of qualification and experience Trainers in many voluntary organisations should be able to apply for this Accreditation (as a counselling skills trainer) when the full scheme is introduced. In the meantime it will be helpful to look at what might make an effective trainer in a voluntary setting. It should come as no surprise to trained listeners and counsellors that the following qualities are desirable when attempting to enable the personal development of volunteers during training (in addition to being good at the organisational side of putting on training events):
- empathy,
- a non-judgmental approach,
- acknowledgement of the intrinsic value of each human being,
- emotional and cognitive sensitivity,
- integrity and congruence - the sense of personal wholeness, honest communication and being consistent,
- impartiality - to endeavour to be aware of their own position in relation to religion, gender, sexuality, race, physical ability, age, nationality, party politics, social standing, class or any other cultural factors and to ensure that their work with clients is not diminished by partiality,
- respect - valuing each trainee's individual way of responding.

The responsibilities of being a trainer/group leader include:
- drawing up aims and objectives for the course as a whole.
- clearly identifying what model of training will be used. (If, for

example, you are aiming for a self help model, then your responsibilities will be related to encouraging self help and mutual support within the group.)

• setting limits and accurately defining responsibilities. (The trainer will need to set limits for him/herself and to help the group do the same. These limits are sometimes called ground-rules.)

Guidelines for effective learning

Being a facilitative trainer has particular implications for the way training happens. A facilitative approach is more congruent with a helping agency since it *enables* rather than *directs* the trainees. The skills required to facilitate active learning would include:-

• giving positive feedback,
• being supportive and challenging in appropriate measures,
• being warm rather than cold and distant,
• being a good listener,
• valuing participants contributions,
• being non-judgemental,
• using open ended-questions,
• using affirmative statements which inspire confidence rather than put-downs which undermine it,
• being flexible and optimistic,
• admitting mistakes,
• making use of humour,
• respecting confidentiality.

When time and resources are limited, learning is more efficient when people have clear objectives towards which they can direct their learning. They will need to know:

• what you expect them to learn from each session,
• how the session fits into the overall course,
• how the course will equip them with skills to do the work.

These can be achieved by recapping learning at the beginning and end of each session, and making the learning concrete by asking if they have been able to tie anything covered on the course into their everyday lives.

It is important to acknowledge that people learn in different ways, some prefer to see pictures or be shown, some like to hear or be told and some like to practice and have a go. It has been said that we learn 20% of what we read, 30% of what we hear, 40% of what we say, and 90% of what we see, hear, say or do, so use a variety of methods. If you have never done any training before you may not realise how simple the message needs to be kept. Curiosity and interest need to be aroused and maintained, so to open the learner's mind and not bore them to death, keep individual talks short, twenty minutes maximum. Use visual aids to emphasise key points. Facilitate discussion by asking questions, 'Does that make sense to you?' and 'What do you think/feel about that?'

As the course proceeds, it is important to monitor learning to discover whether the trainees are actually learning anything. Given that the same words can have different meanings for people, various forms of feedback are needed in order to tell us whether the subject is being understood.
  • Ask trainees to discuss issues and listen to the discussion carefully to see if they have understood.
  • Get trainees to demonstrate the skills which you wish to be learned. This also helps develop skills since people learn by doing and develop skills by doing them often enough.
  • Provide opportunities for thinking, talking and problem solving.
  • Be prepared for strong emotions that can block learning, allow people to express their feelings, be interesting and don't forget that learning is, in this setting, a peer relationship, so you will have to develop mutual respect.

Evaluation
Evaluation is essential if you wish to measure how effective the training has been when the course is finished. Evaluation attempts to answer questions like, 'What did the training accomplish?' 'Of what value were these achievements?' In addition don't forget to evaluate your role as a trainer. Finally, do remember that there is probably no such thing as the perfect course.

Guidelines for evaluation
- Prepare an evaluation sheet for each session. Try to find if each set of learning objectives has been met, session by session.
- Be prepared to feel let down if you hear that learning has not been absorbed. You will need to know reasons for this.
- It is worth finding out what stopped the learning process. Was it for one person or the whole group? Can the blocks to learning be removed?
- Do any of the learning objectives need to be changed?
- Use questionnaires to measure the perceived quality of the course.

You can judge the success of the course if the trainees have learned the basic principles and can apply them, their willingness towards learning more, and finally their appreciation that training is only the first step.

If the course has been unsuccessful for a course participant, you need to be clear in your own mind what the person has not learned and why this course has been unsuccessful for that person. Be factual, clear and precise about what was done or not done. If a person does not meet the standards you have set in order to be telephone helper/listener try the following steps:
- Arrange a meeting with your co-trainer to discuss any problems encountered. (You should have been doing this anyway to nip any potential problems in the bud.)
- Arrange an interview and explain your decision to the trainee. (See page 190 on 'Counselling-out')
- Make a statement at the beginning of training that attending the course does not automatically guarantee being taken on as volunteer.
- Give clear guidelines as to the number of sessions needed to attend e.g. if a volunteer misses more than three sessions, then they would need to join the next training event.

My experience has been that self-selection is the best method of ensuring on-going commitment. If they are not suitable, most volunteers diagnose this themselves and drop out at an early stage as they come to realise that the course is not for them. The session on

'Prejudices and belief systems' has been a good indication of suitability for a number of trainees.

Training at Family Contact Line
Criteria for selection or rejection
At FCL we consider selection to be a two-way process. Prospective volunteers need to know about our particular agency and whether they would like to work for us, and we need to assess if the volunteer will be of benefit to the agency.

Volunteers will need information on:
- how and why the organisation started,
- the aims of the organisation,
- the commitment required (time for training and duties),
- details of how the organisation works,
- the preparation course,
- the selection procedures.

It is also useful to give as much written information as possible in order to make it absolutely clear to applicants, this can be in the form of leaflets and/or agency policies. At FCL we are looking for volunteers who:
- show tolerance,
- are warm receptive and caring,
- have respect for other people,
- are genuine and open,
- are willing to examine their own thoughts, feelings and reactions.

Volunteers without these qualities will have difficulty being open to the personal learning necessary and have a potential to damage the caller, the group and themselves if they are allowed to join the agency.

The interview
The interview itself will be a series of dilemmas for which there is no help since the answers will depend upon the type of service your agency is offering. Do you choose the anxious volunteer or the confident one? If a volunteer seems very anxious it may be because they are fearful of the responsibility of being a helper. You need to

explore these feelings and explain that they will not be expected to have all the answers nor to take responsibility for other people's problems. If a volunteer seems very confident and 'knows all the answers' then they need to be told that this will not help the caller, who need to find their own solutions.

Having set your objectives and elicited help from your fellow trainers or training committee, procedure guidelines need to be set out to help define the interview process. It is good practice to have more than one interviewer present. Two views of the volunteer can be thrashed out in discussions afterwards and the responsibility of accepting or rejecting a particular person does not fall on one team member's shoulders.

Guidelines for interviews
- Make interviewee as comfortable and relaxed as possible.
- Seating arrangements should not be intimidating or threatening to the interviewee.
- Break the ice by introducing interviewers and by giving information about how the interview will be conducted.
- Ask the same questions of every interviewee.
- Ask questions in the same order with the same person asking each question.
- Ask additional clarifying questions only to elicit relevant factual information.
- As far as possible treat each interviewee in the same manner.
- Keep to time.

An application form for volunteers could be sent prior to interview enquiring how they found out about your agency and reasons for wanting to join. Also whether they know any agency member, together with their professional/voluntary experience. Applicants statements should be in line with the broad aims of the organisation and its training. The training aims at FCL are to establish trust, to focus on self awareness and to develop and facilitate learning. Trust will grow with openness and honesty within the group and a feeling of safety and commitment from each member. Self awareness is not just how people respond to issues like abortion, child abuse, etc. but the knowledge that all of us will feel differently because of our different childhood and adult experiences. Respect for each individual's differences is fostered and learning to broaden our own experiences is encouraged by sharing the experiences of others and by sharing our experiences with them. We look for the potential for these qualities in applicants.

The next step at FCL was to formulate a training manual, our own agency document, listing contents and giving session by session breakdown of what we hoped each session would achieve.

Examples of two training sessions at FCL
Session 1 Introduction
  • Establish ground rules and set guidelines designed to help the group work together in a satisfying way. Ground rules ensure that participants and facilitator know what is expected of them. Ground rules might include:
    • Everyone accepts responsibility for their own learning.
    • Everyone listens to each other.
    • Everyone respects confidentiality.
    • No-one is required to reveal information about themselves they don't wish to.
    • Being non-judgmental and accepting other people's viewpoints.
    • Valuing every participant's contribution.
    • Practical issues such as time-keeping, smoking, coffee breaks, etc.
  • Format of course, preparation for training; rules and regulations e.g. punctuality, attendance, homework, etc.
  • Who we are and how we got started. Aims and objectives of FCL, how we operate, where we see ourselves going.
  • Introduction of each member in pairs and present partner to the group saying a little about who they are and why they want to join FCL.
  • Discuss how this felt; this is the first step to listening.
  • Qualities needed to be a good listener (Flip Chart)
  • Requirements of effective listening and understanding ourselves as a listener.

This is an information giving session, the beginning of the method of self selection in which participants can decide whether FCL is going to be right for them. Questions and discussion are encouraged at all stages of the training and in this first session it is important to set the right atmosphere.

Session 2 Prejudices
  • Feedback from the previous session.
  • Discussion on why we should get to know ourselves better. Look at the prejudices to enable a better response to the client.
  • Prejudice questionnaire asking for an 'immediate' response. Asking that trainees avoid 'don't know' if possible.
  • Collect tear off slips and collate information.
  • Case study discussing a wife and mother who discovers her husband is gay.
  • Give results of questionnaire.
  • Trainees split into groups with an established volunteer as discussion leader.
  • Further discussion this time as a large group. Were there any surprises, any change of opinions since doing the questionnaire and individual group discussion.
This is the session in which we begin to *know* the new trainees better - their attitudes, qualities, flexibility and ability to see another point of view.

Further examples of course contents include sessions on:
Listening skills, positive aspects of counselling, pitfalls of counselling, self-awareness, bereavement and loss, child abuse including sexual abuse, the FCL referral book and referral procedures.

After the training course
Once volunteers have met the requirements of the course and agree to go on rota they are assigned to their rota of choice and come under the guidance of the Rota Leader whose responsibility is to induct the volunteer into the everyday workings of the centre, to meet with other members of the team to ensure good practice is maintained. The main focus is to listen to how existing volunteers respond to calls and when the volunteer feels ready, to take a call under the

supervision of the rota leader. After eight weeks of listening a feedback training session is held for discussion. This, 'How are things going?' meeting is an opportunity to reflect upon the training, its effects and the first eight weeks of office experience in which trainees have 'shadowed' experienced volunteers. Trainees can bring any problems, anxieties or joys experienced, and will be told of the ongoing training FCL expects new volunteers to commit themselves to, including sessions on:

• The purpose of support meetings and supervision.
• Writing of case sheets - help and discussion.

Counselling-out

When a volunteer fails to meet the requirements of the course, we feel it is important to seek consultation with, and the support of, colleagues and our Training Committee. The volunteers will have been informed at the beginning of the course about the method of selection, therefore, have some understanding that not being accepted is a possibility. However, knowing this will not necessarily make it easier for the volunteer. At FCL we try to follow these guidelines:

• Be prepared to give factual feedback on the trainees' behaviour during the training period and the reasons for being unsuccessful as decided by the training team.
• Be kind but firm, make sure you hear their point of view and give positive feedback first.
• If appropriate, encourage the applicant to consider other kinds of voluntary work.
• Inform the rest of the group who may be upset (and this may need to be acknowledged). You do not have to give personal or detailed explanations.
• At the outset all trainees should know that the trainers have a responsibility to ensure that callers receive the best possible service.

And finally

Training policy and process at FCL is always developing. In fact it will probably, as a process of our continual review, have changed as you are reading this. Forever juggling resources such as time and money, assets such as the generous goodwill of our volunteers, and the needs of our local community is something that we will never get right. Anyone who decides to organise a voluntary telephone helpline will discover this for themselves. I have finished off by including a piece (on page 192) written by a new volunteer which we included on the FCL Annual Report for the years 1992/3. It summarises the terrors and joys of helpline work and is testimony to the work of thousands of telephone volunteers throughout the world.

Trainee volunteer report
(As cited in FCL 1992/3 Annual Report)

Somebody once said that the problem with early retirement was early retirement (to bed) because you had nothing to do. The advice was to try doing something for nothing instead, so turning your loss into a gain. For me, after an abrupt end to a thirty-four year professional career, one of my gains has been to train and work as a volunteer with Family Contact Line. I will never forget taking my first telephone call. What would I say? They may not want to talk to a man. What if....?

Ring...ring   Where did I put my training notes?

Ring...ring   What were we taught?, Active listening, Empathy, and being Nonjudgemental.

Ring...ring   I remember the course said answer the phone after the third ring: 'Family Contact Line. May I help you?"

Forty minutes later (it seemed like only ten) the caller had rung off saying, 'Thanks, you've been a great help.' Helped? - I felt so inadequate. The training, which was both excellent and enjoyable, had said:

Don't give advice	so I hadn't.
Don't criticise	so I hadn't.
Don't be shocked	so I wasn't.
Don't moralise	so I hadn't.
Don't give your opinion	so I didn't.

But, I had listened...and listened...and listened, paying full attention and encouraging the caller as they struggled to tell their story. This was no training scenario; this was a real call, a real person, a real problem and real emotions. They had reached 'the end of the line' and needed to talk to someone at the end of the (telephone) line.

Every telephone call was a learning experience for me and as a 'new boy' I regard myself as 'on probation ' - the 'trainee' kind, not the 'offender' kind, although I have to confess to feeling that many times my sentence is 'suspended' as I listen to callers.

Martin 1992

Appendix

References

Barry C. Barman (1980) 'Therapeutic Management of Chronic Callers to a Suicide Prevention Centre', *Journal of Community Psychology*, Vol.8, pp45-48.

British Association for Counselling, *Code of Ethics and Practice for Counsellors* (1992 Amended AGM 1993).

British Association for Counselling, *Code of Ethics and Practice for Counselling Skills* (1989).

R.R. Carkhuff (1969) *Helping and Human Relations* (2 volumes), Rinehart and Winston.

P.K.G. Davies (1982) 'The Functioning of British Counselling Hotlines' *British Journal of Guidance and Counselling*, Vol. 10, No. 2.

Gerard Egan (1975) *The Skilled Helper*, Brooks-Cole (and later editions.)

Jennifer Hinson (1982) 'Strategies for Suicide Intervention by Telephone', *Suicide and Life Threatening Behaviour*, Vol.2, No.3.

Family Contact Line (1992/3) *Annual Report.*

Andrew R. Hornblow (1986) 'Does Telephone Counselling Have Preventive Value?' *Australian and New Zealand Journal of Psychiatry*, Vol. 20, pp23-28.

Patricia A. Hunt (1993) 'Relateline: an Evaluation of a Telephone Helpline Counselling Service for Marital Problems', *British Journal of Guidance and Counselling*, Vol.21, No.3.

Francesca Inskipp (1986), *Counselling: The Trainer's Handbook, 'The Effective Trainer Series'*, National Extension College.

Francesca Inskipp and Brigid Proctor (1993) *Making the Most of Supervision*, Cascade.

Francesca Inskipp and Brigid Proctor (1995) *Becoming a Supervisor,* Cascade.

David Lester and Gene W. Brockopp (1970) 'Chronic Callers to a Suicide Prevention Center', *Community Mental Health Journal*, Vol.6. No.3.

Stanley Milgram (1963) 'Behavioural Study of Obedience', *Journal of Abnormal and Social Psychology*, 67, pp75-88.

Stephen Murgatroyd (1985) *Counselling and Helping*, BPS/Methuen.

Carl Rogers (1957) 'The Necessary and Sufficient Conditions for Therapeutic Personality Change', *Journal of Consulting Psychology*, Vol.21, No.2, pp 95-103.

Carl Rogers (1961) *On Becoming A Person,* Constable.

Janice Russell, Graham Dexter, & Tim Bond (1992) *Differentiation Between Advice, Guidance, Befriending, Counselling Skills and Counselling,* Advice, Guidance and Counselling Lead Body.

Sanders, P. and Liptrot, D. (1993)*An Incomplete Guide to Basic Research Methods and Data Collection for Counsellors.* PCCS Books.

Sanders, P. and Liptrot, D. (1994) *An Incomplete Guide to Qualitative Research Methods Counsellors.* PCCS Books.

Linda Viney (1983) 'Experiences of Volunteer Telephone Counselors: A Comparison of a Professionally Oriented and a Non-professionally Oriented Approach to Their Training.' *Journal of Community Psychology,* Vol.11.

Steven Walfish (1983) 'Crisis Telephone Counselors' Views of Clinical Interaction Situations', *Community Mental Health Journal,* Vol.19, No.3.

Steve Williams, (1993) *An Incomplete Guide to Referral Issues for Counsellors,* PCCS Books.

Further reading

These titles have been selected on the basis of their being designed to give practical help, to be interactive or to provide training, rather than simply to be academic texts. There has been little published on telephone helping and telephone counselling, but the British Association for Counselling is an excellent general resource for helpers and counsellors, whatever the setting. The Annual Training Conference is held in September of each year and provides a range of workshops run by experienced counsellors and trainers. It is also a great opportunity to meet like-minded people.

Telephone helping

Telephone Helplines, Guidelines for Good Practice, 2nd Edn, Telephone Helplines Group, 1993, available from Resource Information Service, see below.

Helpline Evaluation, Guidelines for Helplines Seeking to Conduct an Evaluation of Their Service, Telephone Helplines Group, 1995, available from Resource Information Service, see below.

Telephone Helplines Directory published by the Telephone Helplines Association. Available from Resource Information Service, see below.

Counselling skills

If you have no formal training in counselling and want to learn more about basic counselling skills, try:

First Steps in Counselling by Pete Sanders, 1994, PCCS Books.

This book is written for introductory courses of around 10 weeks (20-30

hours training). It is a good companion text for agency training in basic skills. For more counselling skills training up to certificate level (one evening a week for a year, around 100-130 hours) try:
Next Steps in Counselling by Alan Frankland and Pete Sanders, 1995, PCCS Books.
For more detailed discussion of referral:
An Incomplete Guide to Referral Issues for Counsellors, Williams, S., 1993, PCCS Books.

Resources for trainers
Counselling: The Trainer's Handbook, Francesca Inskipp, 'The Effective Trainer Series' published by the National Extension College.
This manual is essential reading for all would-be trainers and also will be of help to experienced trainers.

Supervision and supervisee skills
Making the Most of Supervision, Francesca Inskipp and Brigid Proctor, 1993, Cascade.
Becoming a Supervisor, Francesca Inskipp and Brigid Proctor, 1995, Cascade. Available from Cascade, 4 Duck's Walk, Twickenham, Middx.

Research methods and skills
An Incomplete Guide to Basic Research Methods and Data Collection for Counsellors, Sanders, P. and Liptrot, D., 1993, PCCS Books.

Organisations & contacts
British Association for Counselling, 1 Regent Place, Rugby, CV21 2JP.
Telephone Helplines Group - will, in March 1996 become the:
Telephone Helplines Association, (ESG) PO Box 7, London, W5 2GQ.
Resource Information Service, The basement, 38 Great Pulteney Street, London, W1R 3DE. (Suppliers of Telephone Helplines Association publications).

Leaflets & other resources
Becoming a Counsellor: A Guide to Training in Counselling and Psychotherapy, by Hetty Einzig, pamphlet published by BAC.
Counselling, Confidentiality and the Law, by Tim Bond and BAC Standards & Ethics Sub-Committee, pamphlet published by BAC.
Calling Helplines, leaflet produced by The Telephone Helplines Association.
Need to Talk, leaflet produced by BT. Also gives a Freefone number for information on calling confidential helplines: 0800 0800 08.

Index

Index

Other Titles from PCCS Books

The Steps in Counselling Series

FIRST STEPS IN COUNSELLING by Pete Sanders

The highly acclaimed, best-selling companion for all those involved on Introduction to Counselling Courses. This book is written, and laid out in order to engage the reader, its personal style adds to its accessibility.

NEXT STEPS IN COUNSELLING by Alan Frankland & Pete Sanders

The sequel to the above book, written in the same approachable style but designed to be more challenging for those studying on Counselling Skills courses. Fictional characters are used to illustrate skills and their appropriate use.

STEP IN TO *STUDY* COUNSELLING by Pete Sanders

For all those returning to study counselling at both Counselling Skills and Diploma levels. All aspects of assessment are covered including making and reviewing tapes, writing essays, keeping journals etc.

AN INCOMPLETE GUIDE TO REFERRAL ISSUES FOR COUNSELLORS
by Steve Williams

Steve Williams tackles the problem of how to make, or receive, principled, satisfactory referrals; how to recognise when you need to make a referral and why. A useful book for students, trainers and practitioners.

PERSON-CENTRED APPROACHES IN SCHOOLS by Jackie Hill

The book teachers have been waiting for to complete their training. This text contains the blue-print for a way of being in schools that values and respects the individual, making suggestions for tackling the long-standing problems of bullying, poor motivation, truancy, aggression etc.

EMERGING WOMAN by Natalie Rogers

This book, first published in the United States, tracks the personal and creative development of Natalie Rogers who, along side her famous father, has made a considerable contribution to the world of person-centred growth through expressive arts.

The Counselling Research Trilogy

AN INCOMPLETE GUIDE TO BASIC RESEARCH METHODS & DATA COLLECTION FOR COUNSELLORS by Pete Sanders & Damian Liptrot
AN INCOMPLETE GUIDE TO INFERENTIAL STATISTICS FOR COUNSELLORS
by Damian Liptrot & Pete Sanders
AN INCOMPLETE GUIDE TO QUALITATIVE RESEARCH FOR COUNSELLORS
by Pete Sanders & Damian Liptrot

This trilogy of books on the subject of counselling research is designed with the first-time, or timid, researcher in mind. It uses clear language and counselling examples to guide the new researcher step-by-step through their research. The books are even fun to read

Counselling Research Files

CHILDHOOD SEXUAL ABUSE, SEXUALITY, PREGNANCY & BIRTHING - A Life History Study *(Counselling Research File No.1)* by Patrica Smith

The first in a new series of research monographs, this book makes the connection between childhood sexual abuse and its effects on the sexuality and child-bearing of one woman. It is a fine example of counselling's increasingly popular qualitative research method.

How to order books

Available at a discount direct from PCCS Books. Further discounts available for orders of 10 or more books.

Write/phone/fax: **PCCS Books**, Paragon House, 48 Seymour Grove, Old Trafford, Manchester, M16 0LN. Tel 0161 877 9877 Fax 0161 877 9878